Sara Thurman

Small Beginnings
A Journey to the Impossible

Cover design, interior layout and formatting: Ashley Davis
Editor: Annie Laurie Ward
Studio Photography: Christin Hume

Printed in the U.S.A.

ISBN: 9781734156010
Library of Congress Control Number: 2019914606

To Wayman
the strong, wise and gentle wind beneath my
wings who is my voice of love

In Memory of Hugh and Olga Coston
Daddy and Mama, for always believing in me and
gifting me the courage to carry on your legacy of love

And also for you
because through my story, God speaks to the
steps inside your own

Contents

Introduction

> "Do not despise these small beginnings, for the LORD rejoices to see the work begin, to see the plumb line in Zerubbabel's hand." Zechariah 4:10 (NLT)

The way God orchestrated our creation, His image in us to love Him and love others, initiated a sacred story to be told. It is a story that plants seeds in fertile ground. It is a story to inspire us to reach for the unknown.

God's power continues to cultivate His design of who I truly am in this encompassing creative journey. It started small and did not happen overnight. But it is my powerful story of hearing God, surrendering and moving toward something that I could not yet see. Not everyone will have the same journey, but I hope that part of my story can inspire you to start and to take the next step.

In July 2017, My Man and I were camping in the Lincoln National Forest near Cloudcroft, New Mexico. I kept hearing, *"Write a book about your story — the story of becoming an artist."* I heard this in my spirit and knew it was God speaking to me.

I responded with my hand on my hip, *"God, if you want me to write this book, then You have to tell me what You want in this story."* Within three hours I had journaled the ten chapter titles for this book. Specifically, it was the steps He was unfolding in front of me for becoming an artist and starting a small business. God told me to share with you what He was teaching me. This is not only for an artist but for anyone who has a dream and wants to see the impossible happen. This book is for you. The fact that God gave me the chapter titles that day, in the middle of the forest, was enough confirmation for me to know He had given me an assignment to write! But life went on. I painted, and for the next year I did not write anything else for the book.

Then, in July 2018, I heard specific instructions from God, *"You need to write right now. The small beginnings story needs to be told. Now."* And so I started writing with intention in August 2018. I could never do this without my God breathing life into my daily walk with Him. I believe He wants you to read our story.

Putting this together in book form has been like weaving a blanket, with each strand being a small thread woven to tell the seasons of my life. They are not always chronological, not always beautiful. If you look underneath you will see some messy loose ends. You will likely even see some missed stitches and broken threads.

This book has your story in it, too. God wants to speak to your heart through the holy intersections of people I have met along the way. Their stories are poignant. I hope that when you see the top side of my woven story you will be inspired and encouraged. God wants to weave your story by using the first step of something that seems impossible, one thread at a time, choice by choice, intertwined with His never-ending grace and love, to create your tapestry.

chapter
one

Your life is a series of small beginnings.

Dream the Impossible

It took me at least one year of painting for me to easily say *"I am an artist."* During that year, it felt like a lie. I didn't really believe it in my inner soul, much like a man named Gideon. An angel came to tell him, *"GOD is with you, O Mighty Warrior,"*[1] while he was hiding and before he fought a single battle. And God called me an artist before I sold one painting. My impossible calling is now my reality—today, I am an artist, just as God told me I was. He told me who I was before I was able to see it with my own eyes.

The Tapestry of My Twenties

I wanted to discover the world beyond my little southwest Texas ranching community where I grew up. In my twenties, something in my spirit had me attracted to adventure and world travel. Yes, I was attending college, but in between every adventure I dreamt and planned the next trip to see the world. Friends often asked me how I could afford to go on so many trips. Where there is a will, there is a way. I knew how to work hard and focus on a goal until I achieved it. I worked waitressing jobs and even worked in maintenance at a nearby state park to fund my next plane ticket. When I saved enough money, I would put my life on hold and take every trip across the Atlantic that presented itself.

I went to Europe twice with just my backpack. I stayed in hostels and rode on trains. My sister and I bought the book *Europe On Ten Dollars a Day*. The book became ragged after six weeks in my backpack with our EuroRail and BritRail passes. We slept on the trains overnight and ended up in a new city to explore the next day. We decided which city and country to go to next, and we adventured over an eight week period.

---

[1] Judges 6:12 MSG

My impossible calling is now my reality— today, I am an artist, just as God told me I was. He told me who I was before I was able to see it with my own eyes.

This Texas ranch girl, who talked with a real Texas accent, was experiencing things that seemed impossible just a few years prior. From spending an amazing five days in the Mediterranean city of Nice, France, to exploring the fiords of Bergen, Norway, we got a taste of Europe. And we really did stay on the budget of ten dollars a day.

Two trips to Israel laid a foundation of awe and respect for the Holy Land. I participated in an epic archeological dig in the Old City of Jerusalem one summer. I learned what it was like to be immersed in a new culture while studying ancient cultures more than 2000 years old. For a brief time, my reality was to wake before dawn, eat pickled fish and cucumbers for breakfast on a kibbutz, and then go to the dig site to sift through gallons of dirt. We were looking for ancient artifacts dating to 400 BC.

My passion was adventure. The world was mine to explore. My parents were the brave ones, actually. They released me time after time to go see the world without the internet and cell phones for sharing information of our wellbeing. Our communication consisted of postcards and an occasional landline phone call every few months. The correspondence systems of today allow almost immediate communications around the world. That was not our reality while traveling in the late 70s and early 80s.

Next was cycling through New Zealand. I had a bicycle accident about two months before I left while on a training ride in Texas. A dog came running out to greet my bicycle, and I ended up on the pavement with road rash on my face, legs and arms. As a result of this biking accident, I developed a fearful heart of a repeated crash while cycling. It took mental perseverance to cycle over 1000 miles with that accident fresh in my mind. Not only that, I didn't even really like cycling. But I wanted to experience New Zealand, so I learned cycling. This trip included extensive cycling of over 100 miles a day on dirt roads with climbing and descending mountains. I was getting some real-life experience in the trenches of the "reap what you sow" principle, learning that fear could not control me. Sometimes I had to push through some unexpected and undesirable circumstances to get to the end goal. In fact, on my first day in New Zealand I thought I was going to die as I came down a very steep mountain on a dirt road at high speeds. I was unsure that my brakes were working on my bicycle. But I did not crash! I can still see the exact place in my mind where I stopped safely at the bottom of the mountain. I had to muster up perseverance at that very moment to get back on my bike and complete that two-week cycling trip successfully.

After the New Zealand bicycle trip came to an end, I flew from Auckland to Melbourne to connect with college friends living in Australia. I stayed to explore Australia for three months until my visa expired.

On yet another trip, my heart was saddened greatly by watching the reality of young Egyptian children working at the early ages of five to ten years old. While exploring Egypt on the back of a camel named Dallas (how ironic that I am from Texas), I became fascinated with the young Egyptian children weaving the rugs out of camel hair. They sat on tiny benches when I toured their "factory." I did not see joy in the creating process in these littles. It didn't seem that they had a choice in what to create. It was decided for them. However, I returned to Egypt some thirty years later to observe artisans weaving beautiful tapestries from recycled cloth collected and cleaned from the trash heaps in Cairo. These women artisans were singing joyfully as they created bags, table coverings, and purses. If I knew where to search in Cairo, I am sure I would still find the little children in compromised situations creating by force as I observed in my early twenties.

I worked as a camp counselor and water skiing instructor in northern Minnesota for seven summers where I also instructed canoeing in the Boundary Waters between Canada and the United States. This fueled my pursuit of adventure. And, in addition, it paid me enough to travel and continue my college education.

My time working outside in nature gave me an appreciation of texture and color that is now evident in my own artwork. Birch trees, water, sunsets and the call of the loon at dusk are still influencing my work.

Determination kept me searching to find myself in a career where my life's purpose embraced both joy and happiness instead of just work. I changed my major in college at least seven times: computer science, fashion design, physical education (I took a bowling class in college and finally near the end of the semester bowled my first game over 100), occupational therapy, psychology, social work. I finally landed on an undergraduate degree in General Studies. This was perfect for me because

I still had made no career decision. In my late teens and into the midst of my twenties I attended thirteen different colleges and universities. I was searching. Yes, I liked a challenge, and apparently, I liked changes.

I was pursuing a career that would help me change the world. And I finally found it. Public education was part of my core value, believing that through educating our children we can usher in a better future. Two of my siblings and I became the first college graduates in our family on both the paternal and maternal sides. Education unlocked a career that was far more than what I dreamt possible. I think it's important to mention that when I was in sixth grade I decided I would NEVER be a teacher. As a student, I experienced belittling and negative behavior from several of my teachers and I decided I would never be one of those people. But God had a different plan. I had to let go of that inner vow and allow God to help me dream the impossible. Becoming a teacher at the middle school level met my need for daily challenges, to say the least. Most days I never knew who or what would walk into my classroom or office. I had a successful career as an administrator at the elementary level, middle school level and

district-wide level in the Texas public school system. Talk about a twenty-four-hour job, a school principal takes the prize. There was no time for art during my 24 year career in education. It never entered my mind that I would or could be an artist.

In the last few years of my twenties, I remember praying a specific prayer, *"Lord, I want the very best husband. I will wait. I would rather be an old maid school teacher and never get married. Please show me the very best husband."*

Then one weekend, the impossible happened. It was a dream that I was not sure would ever happen. I went on a date with a man who was a close friend of my parents. I knew after the first week of dating this man, Wayman Lee Thurman, that I was going to be his wife. I waited for the best and God came through. We were married three months later. Every day I thank God for the gift of being married to such a kind, strong, smart and generous man.

"My Samuel's" Miracle Conception

The gift of life

Adventure and travel call to both of my children, as it did to me. But the reality of having your children live on the other side of the world is difficult. It becomes much easier when I step back and reflect. I can see God's purpose. When I take a perspective of God's amazing plans to share His love all over the world, it gives me peace. Reading scripture and familiarizing myself with His word allows me to have something to cling to in different seasons of life. Releasing my son to tell the Good News in the nations is a piece of my story that goes back to his conception.

There is a story that is similar to mine that can be found in 1 Samuel. Hannah is a young woman in ancient Israel who is unable to have children. Not only that, she is ridiculed for not being able to do so. She pleads and prays with the Lord so much that she is mistaken for being drunk in the temple. In her prayer she says,

> *"Oh, God-of-the-Angel-Armies,*
> *If you'll take a good, hard look at my pain,*
> *If you'll quit neglecting me and go into action for me*
> *By giving me a son,*
> *I'll give him completely, unreservedly to you.*
> *I'll set him apart for a life of holy discipline." [2]*

Wayman and I had been married for nearly five years when our oldest son was conceived. We started trying to have children soon after our wedding day. We both were diagnosed with infertility conditions. After four years of following all the medical protocols, Wayman told me if God wanted to give us a child, He would. We could not continue seeking medical interventions. The doctors told us the next step was in vitro, and we knew this was a choice we could not personally make. Wayman's decision to stop all medical treatment caused me to move into a deep depression, as my greatest desire was to have children. I lost hope.

I prayed Hannah's prayer so many times. She did conceive a son, and in her obedience she sent her son, Samuel, to serve in the temple at age three. I knew if God ever answered my prayers to have children, my children would be His.

---

[2] 1 Samuel 1:11 MSG

In February 1990 I became pregnant. No medical intervention. One can only imagine our joy. God had answered my prayers just as He had answered Hannah's. I knew this child was a special gift and a miracle from God.

About six weeks into the pregnancy I began to have severe pain. We went to the emergency room and the doctors determined that I had a tubal pregnancy. The baby grew in my fallopian tube instead of my uterus. My doctor explained that the baby would have to be removed. He suggested that I go to a well-known doctor in the Houston medical center whose expertise was in laser surgery. My original doctor suggested this surgeon in an attempt to save my fallopian tube. While Wayman drove us the 45 minutes to get to the medical center, I sat next to him unable to stop my tears and with Hannah's desperate prayer continually on my lips.

The doctor performed a new ultrasound at the hospital in the medical center and showed us our baby on the monitor. We already knew his name. "My Samuel" showed up on the monitor in my uterus very near the opening of the fallopian tube. His heart was beating. Everything looked normal. Either God had moved the baby, or the first ultrasound was in error. We knew we had experienced a miracle. God had done the impossible. This baby would live. This child would belong to God to serve Him all his days. The rest of the pregnancy progressed normally and Samuel came into the world perfectly formed.

Years later, when Samuel and his wife, Rachel, told us they were going to Central Asia to live and share Jesus, we did not question the call on their lives. They moved overseas in January 2016. Just as Hannah knew her son, Samuel, was born for a life of serving the Lord, we knew our Samuel would have the same calling. What a privilege God gave us to be his parents. Now our purpose in this season of life is to support our children as cheerleaders and sometimes coaches if they ask us. We have a renewed purpose to help them share Jesus in both behind the scenes and on the field. God had already planned our son to be born before the beginning of time to be a messenger of the love for Jesus.

Twenty months after Samuel was born, our second son, Justin, was born. A perfectly healthy pregnancy and delivery. A second gift from God. Our family was full of joy and purpose in teaching our sons and learning from them.

"How Good Can God Be?"

Seeing God's Goodness through Mama's eyes

Wayman and I took care of my mother the last seven years of her life. She lived with us, moved with us and went where we went. Caring for Mama included many beautiful, yet hard experiences. In the spring of 2014, I retired from the Texas public school systems after 24 years of teaching and administration. Mama's health was stable but not improving. She observed and told me how my retirement had birthed new joy and freedom in my life. One of her favorite sayings, "How good can God be?", became a much repeated phrase of gratitude around our home. I knew in my heart that she would likely pass from her earthly life before she saw 2015. I could hear the whisper of God telling me to enjoy each moment and each day remaining with my Mama.

She could not be left alone for more than 30 minutes, and even that amount of time caused her great anxiety. We started using a pair of baby monitors so I could be outside in the yard or back porch.

My dear friend and artist, Ann Younger, came to visit Mama and spend time with me in April 2014. I found myself going a bit stir crazy and needed something to do with my time after my fresh retirement. But, because of Mama's needs, I needed to be home with her.

Pictured: Sara, Samuel, Rachel, Anapaulina, Justin & Wayman

Ann came to my rescue. She taught me some creative assemblage skills. Ann brought old wood and metal pieces as well as turquoise and gold paint. We even found more treasures in my back yard. She taught me how to create with paper mache and we made assemblage pieces on our back porch. There had been no childhood art classes in my school, so I was creating with paper mache for the first time. I loved making these new assemblages with paper mache and wire.

In my childhood years, my grandmother had taught me to crochet and knit, but I was not a habitually crafty person. I even took a quilting class in my late twenties for a couple of years before my career drove out any spare time of creativity. This time creating assemblage was my first exposure to this type of creativity. It opened a piece of me that I didn't know was residing in my spirit.

I kept making assemblage and paper mache items for the next few weeks. Then, Mama had a stroke and passed into the arms of Jesus on June 23, 2014. I wondered about my next season of life. Now that I was retired and the season of caring for Mama was over, I was not sure what was next for me. I grieved deeply for the next several months after her passing. Knowing her body was healed and that she now danced with Daddy in heaven comforted me, but I still missed her. Deep grief requires holy comfort from above.

When the tears came like a rushing river, I let them flow, regardless of where I happened to be. But God's perfect timing opened new windows of opportunity in the world of art even before I could see it.

Deep grief requires holy comfort from above.

Ann came back to visit me for a few days in September 2014 and we created multiple assemblage pieces of art in the shapes of crosses, angels, hearts and even some abstract pieces in Wayman's workshop. Now creating with a specific purpose, we organized a fundraiser in early October for Samuel and Rachel's long term overseas plans. We served venison tacos, had a house concert with friends playing music and had art assemblage pieces to sell. We raised over $2000 that day to give to Samuel and Rachel as seed money for their long term overseas service fundraising campaign.

During this season, in the fall of 2014, Justin began dating a young woman named Anapaulina. Even with the loss of my Mama, we still had so much to celebrate. Samuel and Rachel soon would go serve internationally and Justin would marry Ana. He brought us another wonderful daughter into our family.

It is amazing to me to think that God used a time of mourning to instill a creative outlet for me. In the midst of fear, tears, and releasing my Mama to Heaven, He sent me my friend, Ann. Something so simple yet powerful. Only through Jesus can death be turned to life, can fear be turned to peace, and something that seems so small be turned into great promise.

Cultivate

My first step in painting

I've obviously never been afraid of venturing into unknown spaces, so something inside of me said, "Yes" to a six week Cultivate class offered at our church in October 2014. This class used art as a way to worship. I wanted to "try art", but I didn't know what I didn't know. On those Tuesday mornings, we would first circle up and briefly share where we were in our heads— our current emotional and spiritual status. Then one of the facilitators would share a scripture from the Bible and do a short teaching on that passage. We would meditate on that scripture for a few minutes quietly, then we would move to our individual spots around the room or outside on the porch and start painting. We had no instruction on how to paint besides to engage in the process that God wanted. We talked to Him as we worshiped and painted. The emphasis was not the end product, but on what we heard and experienced internally as a process. Our painting was the product of connection with God. We would have about an hour and a half to paint and worship with God individually. Then we came back together as a group to share what our process had been in that particular session.

We had a variety of tools available to us each week. Paint brushes in all shapes and sizes, palette knives, sticks, et cetera. I used them all and eventually fell in love with the palette knife. I loved the look it gave on the canvas, and, just as importantly, they were so very easy to clean compared to the paint brushes. My subjects each week were usually flowers and hearts and crosses. My first Cultivate painting was called "Tongues of Fire", with thick acrylic layers from the description of Acts 2 of when the Holy Spirit came down.

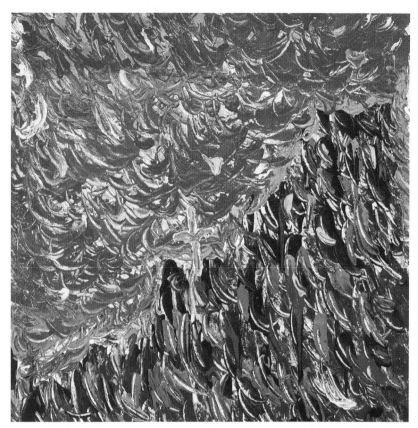

I loved Tuesday mornings, even though I usually cried. I felt ignorant. I felt unskilled. But I pushed the lies away, pushed the walls down that had me boxed in. Fifty-six years worth of not feeling good enough. Fear of being a failure. How could I love Tuesday mornings and be so miserable in my thoughts? It was a battle of my mind. Who was I going to believe?

In the first weeks of Cultivate, I heard that still, small voice. It said to me, *"Sara, you are an artist. An artist for Me."* It was so clear, so out of the blue. It had to have been from the Lord because my own insecurity and disbelief had a hard time accepting it as truth.

I laughed at God and said, *"No way! I have never taken an art class. Why would you call me Your artist? I have no idea what I am doing!"*

And God replied, *"But I do know what you are doing. I know how I created you. Hang out with Me and I will teach you."* So I began to believe that I was an artist for God.

Pictured: "Tongues of Fire"

11

The rest of my time in Cultivate became gymnastics in my mind. My thoughts bounced from believing who God said I was to believing the lies of the enemy that told me I was ignorant for even entertaining the idea. Me, an artist? Yeah, right. Teacher, mother, wife, adventurer, friend. Yes. But artist was not a word that anyone would use to describe me. And retirement was just a bit late in life to start over again in a brand new competitive skilled vocation.

This constant dialogue was such a back and forth frenzy in my mind. And when comparison took over, well, only negative thoughts would fill my mind. *My work was worthless. Other people's work was fabulous. I wish I could paint like them. They are so much better than me. Why am I even doing this? I am wasting my time.* This back and forth conversation was like a battlefield.

The Cultivate environment was set up to protect against such comparison. Our facilitators worked hard and prayed even harder so that there was a safe environment to protect our hearts and souls. They knew we were vulnerable. We were instructed to not compliment other pieces except to say things like, *"your use of color on this piece makes me feel joyful."* Or *"how you used the dark and light takes me to the place of victory."* This allowed for a safe and non-judgemental place to express our creativity. It was this level of safety that gave space for my heart and mind to be willing to continue to paint.

It was as if God took these places of brokenness and made them holy, purposeful. He was healing my wounds.

One week I painted a heart on a large piece of roofing felt, my canvas for the day. I can still remember the exact location of my easel as I painted outside on the covered patio. On this canvas was a picture of my own heart, segmented and broken. It held specific memories of traumatic experiences from my childhood. Designed like a puzzle, with individual colorful jagged edges filling up the heart on a sea of black, it brought back specific images to mind as I drew each piece and chose each color.

Gold paint had never been so sweet or symbolic. The gold became God's healing touch and power. I outlined each piece, each memory, with different colors of paint. It was as if God took these places of brokenness

and made them holy, purposeful. He was healing my wounds. Only God can mend broken hearts. This heart painting was the first time I can remember the holy experience and surprise that God had painted something through me. I had not planned it. Three gold heart shapes were my last three puzzle pieces. It just came out onto the paper with layers of meaning and powerful healing. I could feel something move in my spirit that was new and holy. Cleansing tears made way for life, new life in a new heart.

I had no idea what I was doing most of the time while painting, but it didn't matter. That wasn't the point. The point was worship in the midst of the journey. Embrace the process over product. The point was to go further up and further into who God was and who He said I was.

It would take a week for my pieces to dry because I used so much paint. The layers and texture represented where I was spiritually with God without even knowing it. So much to peel back, to expose. I used excessive amounts of paint because I didn't know any better. I would just begin and see where I ended up.

"God created man in His own image, in the image of God He created him, male and female He created them." [3] This part of the Garden of Eden story out of Genesis 1 changed my perspective about creativity. I never really believed this part of God's story. I was created like the Creator and therefore made to create. Really? I believed that artists were born with an already innate and active artistic ability. I really had believed that not everyone was creative. The truth is that we all are. Each of us is designed with the intention to create. This was a new mindset and perspective for me. It won't look the same, and shouldn't look the same. How boring would that be if we all sat down and painted the same painting, or sang the same song, or wrote the same story?

---

[3] Genesis 1:27 NIV

It was a battlefield in my mind to determine the truth of the whisperings of God regarding my calling as an artist. I would believe I was an artist and move in that truth. Then I would doubt and believe the lie that I was not equipped. It was true whether I wanted to believe it or not. Gideon was a warrior. Hannah was a mother. Sara was an artist. A turning point occurred for me in my identity and my Cultivate friends witnessed this unveiling before their eyes as I became an artist for God.

Mongolia September and October 2016

The first ever service trip together

After months of planning, training, fundraising and trusting, Samuel and Rachel began their life overseas in Mongolia. We planned our first big trip overseas for the fall of 2016 to visit them in their new home. Traveling to the other side of the globe for eight weeks was a long and costly trip. To help us buy our plane tickets, we had continued making and selling crafted pieces. Some were assemblage art, watercolor note cards, and others were woodworking pieces, like birdhouses and wooden trays. Our desire was to be able to pay for travel expenses by selling what we were creating. Many who work internationally raise funds, just as Samuel and Rachel did. It is a great way for people who stay stateside to be able to serve the nations by giving to those who are called to go. We wanted to do it differently. God provided for us by answering our prayers. We were able to create and then sell our items to pay for this first service trip to Central Asia. It was a sweet taste of what He had in store for us just a few years later.

I heard a clear assignment from God to take acrylic paints and brushes to Mongolia. I was to share the connection of art and worship with the young Believers in the church community where we were involved. I was in the small beginning stages of learning about the Spirit-filled creative processes, but I had such a desire to share my excitement with those we would meet on the other side of the world.

I did not take canvases, but I found some in the capital city, Ulaanbaatar. I found two different stores with canvases and bought them for what we called "Art and Worship Nights" with the new Believers. Usually, ten to fifteen young people would attend, and they quickly experienced the presence of God. Some used acrylic paints for the first time. It was beautiful to witness their joy and creative abilities.

Pictured opposite: Sara and some of the Mongolian creative worshipers.

They almost immediately painted with such depth and power. These young Believers did not give in to insecurity. Without worrying about what others thought or if their creations were any "good", they just went for it. They learned to listen to Holy Spirit and worship God through art without restraint. It was my delight to facilitate this experience with them. I left all the supplies I brought to Mongolia for these Believers to continue having special worship and painting times in their community.

Believing the Impossible

The miracle that changed me forever

When the angel Gabriel came to Mary to tell her that she was the favored one God had chosen to carry Jesus, she responded by asking how that could be possible. She was still a virgin. I love that she didn't argue, she just asked a clarifying question. And Gabriel responded, *"nothing is impossible with God."* [4] When God has a plan, He has made a way that we can't yet see. We still get to partner with Him even if it doesn't make sense. God lays on our hearts the things we should pray for while Jesus intercedes for us in the throne room. [5] *"And the Holy Spirit helps us in our weakness. For example, we don't know what God wants us to pray for. But the Holy Spirit prays for us with groaning that cannot be expressed in words."* [6] Jesus, God and the Holy Spirit, the Holy Trinity, are all working together for our good to talk to us and teach us through prayer.

---

[4] Luke 1:37 NLT, [5] Romans 8:34, [6] Romans 8:26 NLT

We are invited to join in with what They are already doing. But we have to believe and risk at times when we can't see what God sees.

Soon after we arrived in Ulaanbaatar, our son Samuel challenged both Wayman and me to pray for the impossible. To pray for something new. To pray and ask God for something that could not happen in any other way except through God's power. When He answered our prayer we would know that there was no other explanation except that the God of the impossible had heard us and answered us. Wayman and I had experienced God in so many ways in our lifetimes. We knew God to be a God of miracles, protection and provision. This, however, was new. This took us a step closer to the mysteries of God and how He truly gives us the desires of our hearts, even when we didn't know it was a desire. Even when it seemed so good to be true that we didn't think to ask for it.

God already told me two years previously, *"Sara, you are an artist for Me."* But what did that mean? Finally, because of this prompting from Samuel, my miracle baby, I allowed my heart, mind and soul to dream. I painted in journal form, created assemblage pieces, painted watercolors, and painted two intuitive acrylic pieces a few months before this Mongolia mission trip. But what was next? On September 16, 2016, I wrote in my prayer journal, *"Lord, I want to paint and sell small, medium and large paintings for You to give money back to people in need all over the world. And I want to make enough to have $4000 of net profits every month."* I really wanted to sell my artwork. I knew this would be impossible unless God made the way. It was my dream.

I did not tell my family what I had written in my prayer journal. It seemed too far out there, which I guess was the point. But I told God. And I believed He would answer if it was His will. If I was going to enter this brand new competitive world of art and be successful, I needed to be specific. And I needed God's help. Especially if the purpose was to reach the nations.

There was no way my art would sell unless God would do it for me. I look back at that part of my prayer. It was specific. It was to the point. It was written. I BELIEVED. It had purpose beyond myself. These aspects of my written prayer that day were important keys to how God answered my impossible prayer.

My Suggestions

• Take time to reflect and pray and connect with God's impossible for your life. God tells us what to pray. *"And the Holy Spirit helps us in our weakness. For example, we don't know what God wants us to pray for. But the Holy Spirit prays for us with groaning that cannot be expressed in words."* [7]

• Believe!

• Pray for the impossible in agreement with God.

• Write it down, maybe in a journal or as a note. Write it in a place where you will see it again.

Reflections and Action Steps

• What dreams do you have that God has planted that may seem impossible?

• Be specific. Ask God for the prayers He wants you to pray in regard to your impossible dreams.

---

[7] Romans 8:26 NLT

chapter
two

Our legacy is to pass on the beauty we create.

Pursue Purpose

So, why? Why would I raise my children, have a life of adventure, have a career in public education, and then use my retirement to start something brand new? Why not kick back and enjoy? Why not read novels and go out for long lunches with friends? Now, while there is nothing wrong with reading and long lunches, I knew I had an assignment that I could not ignore.

As believers, we also have a "why". What is our motivation and purpose? It is simple — Love Him, love ourselves and love others. But what are our individual details under the love umbrella? To be a light on a hill. To bring hope to the hopeless. To turn ashes into beauty. To grieve with those who are mourning. To pray for those who are lost and need comfort. To dance with Jesus leading the way. It is as true for me as it is for you. This is my purpose, and my impossible prayer is the means that drives me towards my purpose in taking the small steps.

My encouragement to you is to dream with God. As I reflect back on the past few years I can see how God had set me up for success. He awakened my spirit to want to become an artist. Then, as I waited on Him, He answered. He heard my prayers, partnered with me and anointed me. Nothing is impossible with God. Pray the kind of prayers that seem impossible to man and watch God move. That is my story exactly.

Our "Why?"

Everything rests on our purpose

If we don't have a purpose, we will simply wander and then end up asking ourselves, *"What are we doing?"*. In the book of Proverbs, it says

When I attend to what God reveals, I am most blessed.

"If people can't see what God is doing, they stumble all over themselves; But when they attend to what He reveals, they are most blessed." [8] God wants to show us His plans for goodness in every trial and in every season of our lives. Ultimately, our purpose has less to do with ourselves and more to do with what God wants.

God answered my prayer to have children. He then called my oldest and his new bride to the nations. We wanted to support, visit and serve alongside them. So He provided the means for us to do those things. It is so simple and beautiful, at times I can hardly believe this is His plan. My purpose in painting is to help bring the name of Jesus to the nations. And through this story of painting, the name of Jesus has been shared from Fredericksburg, Texas, to Mongolia. When I attend to what God reveals, I am most blessed, and my blessing blesses others.

The Name of Acts 1:8 Blessings

A small step of faith from His Word

When one starts a company, there are many decisions to make. At times, it seems as if they are unending. The name of the business was an easy decision to make because of the deep purposes within the scripture Acts 1:8. It says, *"But you will receive power when the Holy Spirit comes upon you. And you will be my witnesses, telling people about Me everywhere—in Jerusalem, throughout Judea, in Samaria, and to the ends of the earth."* [9] This verse encompasses our purpose. This is why we started the business, and it focuses our attention and intentions each day.

The unique process of working together with Wayman in the business proved to be such a blessing. As a gifted woodworker, Wayman's skill set included making frames for my paintings. This hobby of his started in high school when he made a bookcase and gun rack in shop class. Then, after retirement, he built a 16 foot by 20 foot workshop in our back yard. Wayman loves to create new items with unique features. He makes birdhouses, bird feeders (using wine bottles), wooden trays, coffee tables, platform beds, and frames for my paintings. As our business progresses, the variety and types of wooden frames he creates continues to develop. Every so often he creates some new items to allow his own creativity to have momentum. Picture frames can be a bit mundane.

---

[8] Proverbs 29:18 MSG, [9] Acts 1:8 NLT

20

Our purpose statement for Acts 1:8 Blessings is "creating to bring heaven to the ends of the earth." By selling our art products, we are able to fund our mission trips overseas to be with our children several times a year. We are also able to use our financial profits to help others around the world. Our artwork speaks life and love and hope to others because of His anointing. This is my heart's desire—to make the name of Jesus famous in all the earth. We want to help people in need in our Jerusalem—our small town of Wimberley, throughout Judea—our state of Texas, in Samaria—our United States, and to the ends of the earth—in Mongolia, Russia, China, Central Asia, Uganda, India, Greece, Mozambique, Madagascar, Sri Lanka, British Virgin Islands, and the list keeps growing. This is just the beginning of where we help financially through our net profits. What seemed impossible was made possible because of the faithfulness of God.

Painting in Fredericksburg, Texas at Loca on Main

The small beginning of connecting art and ministry

When Wayman and I first visited with Abbey Henderson [10], our small business consultant, she told us that my artwork would sell well in women's boutiques. This was on January 2, 2017. Wayman remembered her suggestion and took action. I, on the other hand, felt less sure and did not want to move forward with her suggestion for fear of rejection.

I grew up in Rocksprings, Texas, a small ranching community about 80 miles southwest of Fredericksburg. There were 23 in my graduating class, most of whom knew one another since the first grade. So, needless to say, we were a close-knit group. We had our 40th high school reunion in 2016. Wayman remembered my classmate, Tooter, telling us that his wife, Terri, owned a women's boutique in Fredericksburg on Main Street called Loca on Main. There is also a sister store in Concan, Texas called Loca on the Frio.

> *What seemed impossible was made possible because of the faithfulness of God.*

So on January 15, 2017, Wayman needed to go check on a broken water pipe on my stepson's property at Harper, Texas, about 30 miles west of Fredericksburg. Wayman told me to get my paintings loaded up in the pickup and we would stop by the boutique. I told him I didn't want to. I was fearful of being turned down. If I didn't try I wouldn't hear, *"No."*

[10]abbeyhenderson.com

My current fear-based mindset changed when My Man "suggested strongly" to get my paintings in the pickup to take to Fredericksburg. Wayman insisted that I choose some of my paintings to drop off. We took about seven to Loca on Main on our way to Harper. I had not painted any larger than 12x12 at this point, so I chose mostly 5x7 and 8x8. Then, on our way back home after fixing the water pipes, we stopped to see if Loca on Main had accepted any of the paintings to be sold on a commission basis at their store. Terri loved them and kept them all to sell!

What an open door and blessing to have my paintings in this lovely women's boutique in the busy Texas tourist town of Fredericksburg. They charge me a small commission for each piece sold and the commission rate is much less than any art gallery in the area. God literally opened double doors into the second room of their shop. They can be opened for me to paint right there at the storefront. I have sold over 200 pieces of art in the two years my art has been displayed in Loca on Main. Wisdom from our small business consultant helped Wayman to push open the door to this. It truly is the goodness of the Lord to be part of this beautiful store that values God and loves to have my paintings as store decorations for their walls. Win-win situations make for healthy relationships for both businesses. I sell my art and they sell more clothing because of the buzz of me painting at their open double doors.

For two days after Thanksgiving of 2017, I did my first painting live at the storefront. I was exhausted at the end of each of those two days and not sure it was something I could do. It was difficult to paint with people watching me. Was this supposed to be something I was to do on a regular basis— paint in public?

But then, in early February 2018, during one of the many times I asked God, *"What's next?"*, I heard, *"Go back and paint in Fredericksburg."* So, during spring break in mid-March, I tried painting in public again. I learned so much. How to be quiet, how to listen to other's stories and not just tell my own. Yes, I was to share my impossible journey of becoming an artist, but the short

version is many times better than the long drawn out version.

I would hear the whisper of God in my spirit say, *"Come on, Sara, people are walking by and wanting to shop, not just listen to your life history."* As I became braver and more courageous, I also began to listen better. I share what I need to share by hearing God whisper specifics about what to say. It is a heart to heart connection through my art with others God sends along my path. I am to be quiet and hear their stories. In the bigger realm of God knowing all things, He is orchestrating who walks by, who stops and what I am to say. I am amazed as He unfolds my art and ministry through live painting in public.

I love getting to meet my customers and experience how my art affects them. Being in face to face conversations has helped me get to know my customers and be able to paint to meet their needs.

"Interlaced" is the word God has given regarding my artwork and ministry. A few months ago I was having a long dialogue with God about selling my artwork and putting so much energy and time into painting. Was I being faithful to what He wanted with my time and energy? I have been actively involved in prayer ministry for many years. What God has shown me so beautifully in painting at the storefront in Fredericksburg is that it is a form of street ministry. I pray for many of my customers. Sometimes, we are all holding hands on the sidewalk asking God for help in specific areas and also praising Him for His kindness and love. My art business is not in front of or a priority over my ministry. God has woven these two aspects of my life in such an unexpected and mysterious way. Relationships reign over anything else.

Inspiration from other Artists

The only artist I knew growing up was Randy Peyton. He had formal training and a career as an artist. We grew up together, and our parents were best friends. Randy painted with such ease and with a beautiful style using oils. Texas bluebonnets in the Texas Hill Country were his trademark subjects. My parents loved his work and even purchased one of his bluebonnet paintings. This painting is now hanging in my home. But I knew I was not an artist as I was growing up because I was not Randy. But today Randy has inspired me to know I am an artist.

As a self-taught artist, many people ask where I got my inspiration to paint. My earliest memory of appreciating a famous artist was Monet. Looking at his florals and water lilies and use of color always created joy in my soul. When visiting the Paris Museums or New York's Metropolitan Museum of Art, I would not miss walking by Monet's collections. The freedom that Impressionist artists had made me feel like I, too, could be an artist.

In my first few months of painting, I would check out art books from the Wimberley Village Library on Impressionism art and study the paintings. Having seen Monet's Poppy Fields at the Musee d'Orsay several times in person, I studied its beauty and even painted it over a period of six weeks with the help of Suzanne King. Suzanne, a professional artist, provided "Open Studio" time on Tuesday evenings in early 2016 in a nearby town. With her guidance, I completed the painting in the spring of 2016. But I decided I wanted to create my own style and not just try to copy another painting.

On both my Instagram and Pinterest feeds, I follow an artist out of Tennessee, Deanne Herbert. Her angels inspired me to create my own. Using an abstract style and a palette knife as her main tool, Deanne's artwork is soothing and peaceful to my soul. Her artwork continues to motivate my growth as an artist.

Double Fold and Ten Fold—"I Am Always With You"

The power of God's generosity intertwined with His purpose

It was a busy Saturday in Fredericksburg, Texas. I was all set up to paint in front of the shop Loca on Main. Every time I set up here I have countless opportunities to visit with people walking by on the sidewalk.

I had already helped several customers find the right piece of art. In fact, a couple studied my angel paintings in particular. Their eyes fell on an 8x8 gallery wrapped acrylic angel on canvas with lots of purple accents. This piece was in the store display window looking out to the street. The husband asked me the price and I said, "$46." I knew that English was not their first language, as most of the time the husband was translating into Spanish all that I said. I also knew they loved this angel. They went on their way down the sidewalk after I responded with the price.

I looked up about an hour or so later and again this same couple stood on the sidewalk looking at the purple-robed angel in the display window. At this point, I heard God tell me to give them the angel. It was a gift for them. But I ignored that still, quiet voice in my spirit. I got distracted with other customers and brushed off the voice of God. Soon afterward, the husband looked at me and said, *"I will be back next Saturday with more money."* I still did not move to obedience. I was busy with other customers.

Then something really special happened. These same customers returned a third time to the store! What? No one has ever come back a third time to buy something. Yes, many come back the second time, but not a third time. I knew God had sent them back. I ran inside the store and tore the price tag off the purple angel. I rushed out to the sidewalk and handed them the painting.

I serve a God who is full of grace. I felt such love from Father God who had sent the couple back the third time so I could be obedient to His request. I explained to them that this was a gift from God. He told me to give it to them when they were there the second time but I had not acted on God's request. I told them the God of Love sees them and knows them intimately. They accepted the gift and understood God's kindness. His wants so desperately to let us know how much He loves us.

The wife handed her phone to her husband so that he could take a picture of us together with the angel on the sidewalk. Just as the husband took the picture her phone alarm went off. It was 3 o'clock. He then explained that his wife has an alarm on her phone that goes off every day at three o'clock to remind her that God is with her. I told them to turn the painting over and read the name. I had named the painting— "I Am With You Always." We all had tears in our eyes. We experienced a holy moment together. God used that moment as an intersection to remind them of His faithfulness while giving me a chance to practice obedience.

This day was not yet over. Wayman was planning on picking me up from Loca around 6 p.m. We were then going to have dinner with family at a local spot. At 5 p.m., Wayman called me and said he would come closer to 7 p.m. because Justin, our younger son, had killed a black buck

God's amazing grace and purpose were ushered in through obedience that day.

antelope and it would take about an hour to get it onto ice. I was happy to wait, but stopped painting about 6 p.m. and put my paintings up against the storefront to wait. I went to visit with the girls in the store for a short time, then came back out to enjoy the evening in my folding chair. My art sales on this particular Saturday were $450. I was very pleased with the amount and satisfied with what God had done for me that day. I have learned that my success is not in the amount of money in sales but partnering with Him. He brings the people that will buy and I need to be obedient to serve as He leads me.

Many of the tourists in Fredericksburg are there for special events like anniversaries, weddings, birthdays, romantic get-aways, and even bachelorette weekends. As I sat on the folding chair waiting for Wayman and Justin, a bride-to-be and her party came by. The bride became interested in my art leaning up against the store and she found a bluebonnet floral painting she wanted to buy. She also liked my large 24x36 original florals, but none of the paintings had the color palette to match the decor in her new home. She asked if I could paint her one with the same colors of a smaller floral she saw in the window. She wanted a large floral 24x36 with the new colors. She paid for additional paintings she bought from inside the store and the new commission, which totaled over $450. In fact, I named the commissioned painting for the bride and her new home, *"Eternal Love."* She and her husband later hung it in their bedroom.

Later that evening I realized what God had done for me. My original intention was to be packed up by 5 p.m., but the extra time had produced a double fold. I received double the sales of the day. My sales went from $450 to $900.

Then God reminded me about the purple angel I had given away earlier that day. *"I Am With You Always"* was valued at $46. His faithfulness brought me a chance to partner with Him, follow His lead and choose obedience. And what did God do in response? In the last extra hour, He gave me almost ten-fold. My extra sales equaled close to ten times what I had given away. God continues to show me His goodness over and over. I can't out give Him. God's amazing grace and purpose were ushered in through obedience that day.

"Abundant Hope"

A story of portraying purpose beyond the physical canvas

I began painting some new types of florals in spring 2018. Using my palette knife and some complimentary colors, I enjoyed expanding what I was painting. Just a few weeks into painting in public I had a delightful customer buy one of my new florals. *"Abundant Hope"* was a 20x24 acrylic on a gallery wrapped canvas with shades of pinks and greens. Before noon on this particular day, a customer named Marci stopped by and began looking at my artwork. She ended up buying a much bigger painting than she had anticipated.

Since then we have developed a beautiful and lasting relationship. She frequently sends me a message to see when I will be painting in Fredericksburg and has brought friends with her from San Antonio. I have been able to pray for her and her friends on some critical health

Pictured: Marci and Sara with "Abundant Hope"

issues. Because of their purchases, I was able to donate a painting to a fundraiser for a non-profit organization Marci helps with in San Antonio. When she was ready to do her Christmas shopping, she came back to Loca on Main in Fredericksburg.

God is using my art to bring hope and peace to people. The phrase "Abundant Hope" actually became an anthem for Marci. The following is Marci's written testimony of what happened as a result of our meeting and her purchasing *"Abundant Hope."*

> *"It was a warm March day when I decided to take a drive to Fredericksburg for the day. I was feeling down, sad and lonely. I had a rough week and needed to get out and spend some time thinking and reflecting. In some respects, I was lost and had lost hope. And then I found Sara.*
>
> *I found her painting in front of a store and we started chatting. In a short time, she restored my hope with her kindness, prayers, hugs, smile and, most of all, a beautiful painting. It spoke to me immediately and was named "Abundant Hope". Hope became an important word for me as I fought breast cancer 8 years prior to that fateful day. I collected anything with the word "hope", and the painting was perfect for my bedroom.*
>
> *I think God called me to take that walk down the sidewalk to find Sara. It was such a glorious moment! Each time I look at the painting I smile because it brings me such joy and happiness!"*

I am overwhelmed with renewed purpose when I realize how God is bringing His love and light and hope to those who connect with this artwork. I pursue God's purposes and he continues to refuel me for the next step. I am blessed and surprised with each step of my small beginnings.

Reflections and Action Steps

• Write your purpose statement for this season. In each season of life, our purposes may need realignment to God's purposes.

• Think about the three umbrellas: Loving God, Loving Ourselves and Loving Others. Are there any action steps you need to take to be under the covering?

chapter
three

Do hard things.

Create Discipline

Daddy would wake me up before the sun so we could be in the pasture at daybreak ready to round up the sheep, goats or cattle. No matter what season was upon us, we would have to get up and get started.

Daddy always asked me how many eggs I wanted for breakfast. He was the breakfast cook in our house and knew the importance of having fuel for the workday ahead. I usually replied *"None!"*, but he always cooked me at least one. I still don't like the way he cooked eggs—get the skillet hot, break the eggs in and scramble them as they cook. You save washing a bowl that way. And you may get a little extra crunch with a few eggshells.

My Daddy was a hard worker, and through his example, I learned early in my childhood about the sowing and reaping principle. I grew up on a large ranch in southwest Texas where I learned that if you wanted to eat, you had to work. We had a garden as big as a roping area. Actually, it was planted in the roping area. It took all of us working together to have food on the table every night. This was not an instant gratification lifestyle. Everything took time and effort, which lead to a groundwork of discipline in my life.

I would not be an artist today without discipline. When God told me I was an artist for Him, I knew I was not just going to immediately paint pieces of art that people would want to buy. I knew it was going to take discipline and hard work. In fact, it was more than two years of practicing and honing my skills before I started selling art.

When God told me to start Acts 1:8 Blessings, I had to examine my life and see where I was spending time that was not sowing into purposeful and life-giving activities for the business. I had to have time to paint without distractions. Extra activities without purpose towards improving my art were discarded in my daily and weekly routines. These decisions meant more time alone painting and less social activities in my community. It meant sacrifice, and it meant saying no. Learning to use every minute of every day to be in alignment for God's purposes in my life has revamped the structure of how I spend my time.

I love the parable about sowing and watching where you plant the seeds. If they fall on the rocks, the birds will come along and eat the seeds. You want to plant in deep, rich soil, but even then care is needed for the harvest to be bountiful. [11] It requires both watchful and purposeful planting. Growing my ability and skills as a painter, along with expanding the art business, requires constant reflection and improvement. When moving towards excellence, one cannot be stagnant. This honing of skills is dependent on my communication with God. He is the one instructing us on what feels like a moment by moment basis.

I call God my Great Communicator because He is always available to ask for wisdom in my planting and painting. His instruction can sometimes feel like pruning, which brings a greater harvest. And you know, just like my daddy taught me, I have a garden of my own that enables me to experience this first hand. It is good to prune the vines. Don't be afraid to prune deeply. Re-evaluate what is working and what is not. Let peace be your compass. Prune away where there is no fruit. Ask God to show you where to plant and water and fertilize, and then get ready for an abundant harvest. Look to the areas in your life where you have been harvesting fruit and sow more in that zone.

What is God doing today and how can I join in on the action?

One of the characteristics of discipline that God has given me is the insight to just start. Get off the couch. Get away from the computer or cell phone, or Facebook, or Instagram, or whatever distractions rob me from having discipline.

There are also outward signs that we are filled with the Spirit of God. They are called the Fruit of the Spirit, and one of them is self-control. I ask God what changes He wants me to make to be successful. He has told me and will continue to tell me when I ask. It may be to start an action plan. I ask God what He wants to accomplish through me. What is

[11] Luke 8:4-8

God doing today and how can I join in on the action? I dream with God. I write out my goals and do something every day to move me closer to those goals. *"Arise, Sara! Let your light shine for all to see. For the glory of the Lord rises to shine on you."* [12] This verse speaks truth to my heart and moves me forward with God's powerful light.

My First 100 Day Project

A critical key to unlocking creativity through daily practice and discipline

April 10, 2015—Day one of my first 100 Day Project. Having experienced periods of my life sitting under a dark cloud of depression, this day seemed darker and lonelier than most. I was battling for my identity as a loved and known daughter of the Most High King. In the New Testament, Paul explains how the key to renewing your mind is wrapped up in what you think about. [13]

On this particular day, I asked God for help to move me out of this depressed mindset. Almost immediately, while scrolling on my phone, I saw something about The 100 Day Project. I was intrigued in my spirit. As I continued searching on my phone, I found a connection to a TED talk about the power of 100 Day Projects. I listened to the talk right then and committed to a daily practice of creativity for the next 100 days. This answered my prayer and moved me to action. It gave me a focus to be able to get out of my depression and to cultivate new artistic skills.

Participating in my first 100 Day Project absolutely propelled me to succeed as an artist. Committing to a daily practice provided the time and discipline needed to unearth and improve my creativity. So, that very day, I started my 100 Day Project by using an electronic journal application on my iPhone called Day One. This app acted as part of my accountability system so that I was sure to have a journal entry before midnight each day.

Notes from my first entry:

> *"Day one of my 100 day challenge! Create in me a clean heart. Speak to me, God. Holy Spirit, come and settle on me to bring glory to You. I desire Your mind, JESUS. I desire to rest in You and You alone!"*

I even wrote down the guidelines for my 100 days.

---

[12] Isaiah 60:1 NLT, [13] Romans 12:2

"Parameters: Use some type of art process. Create a visual using a verse or passage from the Bible. I can use a verse of my choosing, but some days I need to be challenged to use the KLOVE verse or YouVersion daily verse. It can be a photograph, a pencil drawing, an acrylic, a watercolor, or whatever I might need to use to express my creativity of the Holy Word from God. My sword will be sharpened by the 100 day exercise. Lord, be my strength and may I bring glory to You, God! So today is day one. April 10, 2015. July 18, 2015, is day 100. Lord, I am excited to see what all You teach me in this challenge. Lord, I want Your glory to be my rear guard in this project. Holy Spirit, guide me and teach me Your mysteries."

My first entry on Day One connected to John 15:5 *"I am the vine, you are the branches."* [14] Jesus was instructing His disciples to stay plugged in to Him. What they needed to make it through that day was attainable by simply acting like a branch attached to a greater vine. There was no need to do it by themselves. In fact, just like a branch, they wouldn't survive without staying attached to Him, the life source.

When I plugged in to the Life Source, God began to speak to me and open my eyes and ears to see color and texture in His creation that I

---

[14] John 15:5 NLT

never discerned before. I thought the sky was only blue and the grass was just green. Then, with new eyes in childlike wonder, I started seeing texture for the first time — thick layers within the storm clouds and the intricate details of tree bark. And I begin seeing color — different shades and values of colors. My eyes began to notice shades of purple, grays and whites in the sky. I saw light dancing off green leaves in the trees that started to look silvery white. Observing this whole new world of color, detail and structure in nature became the favorite part of my day. God indeed was opening up His mysteries to me as I prayed on Day One. Any twinge of depression in my thoughts would leave as soon as I moved into my journal entry for the day. I was excited to see what I would discover. It felt like a new beginning. It felt like I was plugged back into the vine.

On Day Eight, which also happened be my fifty-seventh birthday, my husband and I drove to the beach on the Gulf of Mexico to camp with friends. As we waited for the ferry to take us across to Aransas Pass, Texas, I was reading my Bible and discovered a scripture I never remembered reading before. It is found in Zechariah 4:9-10: *"Zerubbabel is the one who laid the foundation of this Temple, and he will complete it. Then you will know that the LORD of Heaven's Armies has sent me. Do not despise these small beginnings, for the LORD rejoices to see the work begin, to see the plumb line in Zerubbabel's hand."* [15] Specifically, verse 10 jumped off the page. This book's name came from this verse. Having never heard the words plumb line before, I asked Wayman the meaning. He told me it is a weight tied to a string for builders to use to be sure the walls are built straight. Everything in the building process is taken back to this line to make sure the foundation, walls, all parts, line up correctly.

Here I was, on Day Eight of this 100 Day Challenge. I was not really an artist. Yet. But yes, I was an artist. I knew I had heard God say I was His artist. I did not know what that meant except to

> *I was not really an artist. Yet. But yes, I was an artist.*

practice my skills. Hang out with Him and His Word every day and ask Him to reveal His mysteries to me. This is still a daily choice of mine. Sowing deep into the soil of God's truth and planting seeds on fertile ground created beautiful fruit and pieces of art.

The idea of a plumb line for my life became so real. The connection to a daily verse increased my focus on God and my rising hope level

---

[15] Zechariah 4:9-10 NLT

affected my greater emotional stability. Every day I took this new season of life that God was building and checked it with His plumb line, His scripture. It was a tool that I could use to always check that I was aligned with His purposes. Depression no longer had a role or a place in my life because I was connected to the vine. I found the true plumb line. He was using these small beginnings to show me a greater purpose through my fingers in order to bring people back to Him. Rarely a twinge of depression raises its ugly head in my thoughts; I can feel it coming. I speak words of truth over myself and hold onto my plumb line of Jesus.

During my 100 Day Project Wayman and I drove to Alaska and back to Texas. This amazing trip was on our bucket list. Over the 16,000 mile road trip, I observed stunning, breathtaking scenery. Day 99 of my journal was penned at Mile 27 of the Alaska Highway where we camped by the mountains near a gorgeous little stream filled with spawning salmon. My scripture and journal entry for the day stated, *"Psalm 34:5 "'Those who look to Him are radiant, and their faces shall never be ashamed' [16] Jesus thank You for healing my soul for restoring me to your fullness of joy!"* Art and photography changed my life. Depression was lifted. God

---

[16] Psalm 34:5 ESV

had opened my eyes to see more of Him, His creation, His love, and His purposes all interlaced with His truth in scripture.

This first 100 Day Project marked an amazing start of God showing me the fruits from the daily discipline of painting and spending time with Him in worship. None of my artwork at this point had been seen in public or sold. It was simply my personal journey with God as He taught me to grow deep roots.

My Beautiful One

An encounter with Truth

Writing is wonderful, empowering, grueling, and tiresome. When God called me to write the story of Acts 1:8 Blessings, He was loud and clear. He told me to write, He gave me the content, and He surrounded me with people I needed. Without question, I knew it was time.

While I was writing the first draft of this very book, Wayman and I decided to take another road trip. My plan was to set aside time during our stay in Maine to write. We were gone for three and a half weeks in October 2018. We don't get much of a Fall season in Texas, so our bucket list got a little more empty during this road trip to the northeast. The leaves, the fresh fish, the layers of clothing and the brisk, cold breeze were everything we Texans' crave. And my self-imposed assignment— write. I had to push myself to get this book out of my head and onto paper. It required discipline.

I had chosen the perfect bed and breakfast on the northern Maine coast to write for four days. But I was struggling. I had a 5:30 am wake up call every morning. This wasn't the front desk calling, oh no. This was the Almighty Himself. And I was getting frustrated. Morning after morning He would wake me up, always at the same time. He'd tell me to get up and get writing. This trip was not about me reading novels and enjoying hours upon hours of sightseeing. I needed to "write right now".

After a few days of this, I said to God, *"I am pretty tired of this book and this assignment. I wish I could just read a novel and not have to focus on Small Beginnings. Like really, who goes on vacation to Maine and has to write?"* Luckily I had a special treat waiting for me each new day. I watched the sun rise up over the Atlantic every morning from our second-floor balcony. He is always good to help with discipline. This particular morning was no exception.

"My Beautiful One," God said as I was waking up.

I replied, *"No, You are my Beautiful One."*

Then God clarified through a quiet whisper, *"No, daughter, you are My Beautiful One."*

I said, *"Well, show me where that is in the Bible and maybe I will believe You."*

I went to Song of Songs 2:10, and there it was. *"The one I love called to me: Arise, my dearest. Hurry, my darling. Come away with Me! I have come as you have asked to draw you to My heart and lead you out. For now is the time, My beautiful one."* [17] I sat in His presence, in awe, crying, watching the sunrise and listening to Him call me *"My Beautiful One"*. It was the song over my life that I needed to hear. It was part of my holy encounter with the One who is writing my story and your story, too.

We need that reminder of who we are. He is our Beautiful One, but we are also His. Just as we want to love on our own children, He wants to do the same to us. Can we receive it? Can we fully embrace who we are to Him? Can we wear our true identity with grace?

He woke me early to watch the sunrise and tell me His love song over my life. Just a week before I had made an encaustic angel in North Carolina. She had a red robe and two turquoise hearts. Now I knew the name and why she had two hearts — one for me and one for Him.

Discipline is worth it when it is God inspired. When He is in the midst of the hard work, it can turn from frustration to blessing. I thought that I was inviting Him into my project, but it was the other way around. He was inviting me into His project. "My Beautiful One", indeed.

The Road of Perseverance

When I think of the times I needed discipline in my life, I cannot help but think of the perseverance it took to complete my doctorate in 1999. Daddy had a vital role in me completing my dissertation.

[17] Song of Songs 2:10

Daddy had been diagnosed with prostate cancer and was seeking medical intervention at MD Anderson Hospital in Houston. Wayman, the boys and I lived in Sugar Land, a suburb of Houston. So my parents came to live with us most of 1999. Daddy lovingly called me his "educated daughter." I wanted to finish my doctorate degree to honor Daddy and to accomplish what I believe God had told me to complete.

I prayed for three months before I made my decision to pursue my doctorate. I was teaching middle school full time. I had two small sons. I was married. And I was to continue going to school to get the EdD? God showed me *"Yes"* as I received confirmation from every direction, including heaven. It was time to reap what I had sown over long years of night classes and weekend classes and papers and exams, and on and on, for five years since finishing my Master's Degree. Daddy set an example for me. In our family, we finished what we started. He never quit. So, as his daughter, the youngest of his seven children, I would not quit, either. I had to finish. But I had to have God help me.

You may have heard of the term, "ABD" which means "All But Dissertation." Many graduate students are ABD. The course work is completed, but the dissertation gets one stuck. My university required me to keep paying them a fee every semester that I had not completed my dissertation. This was to keep my committee members abreast of my progress, as they were university professors. I needed to finish what I had started. I had huge barriers in front of me. I was not sure I could do it. I had to make a plan of discipline to gain momentum again — One step, then another step.

The course work for a doctorate is grueling, but the real discipline comes while working on the dissertation— when you are doing the research and writing each of the chapters, meeting with the committee, following their recommendations, then completing the final steps to publish. Some of my largest boulders were the time needed to complete the dissertation, as well as the interpretation of my research through the statistical programming needed to analyze the results. How would this be possible while working full time, raising two small sons, honoring my husband and trying to do this in my "free time"? It was overwhelming, as I had to run the statistics of my surveys (centered around parent involvement in Title One schools in Texas) I had gathered. I was using a certain statistics program and needed to hire a consultant to help me run and interpret the results.

God helped me find a consultant to program and interpret my survey statistics. God sent me an editor to help me "clean up" my writing. God sent me cheerleaders—my family, including Wayman, my sons, Samuel and Justin, age seven and nine, and Daddy and Mama. Somehow I found the time to complete the dissertation in August 1999. I knew God had made the way.

We went out to eat to celebrate on the day I took the final copies to the university print shop for official publication. Daddy was so happy for me. I was Dr. Sara Thurman, his educated daughter. However, he was so weak from cancer ravaging his body that he was unable to attend my celebratory dinner.

Ten days after I turned in my final copies of my dissertation Daddy passed from this earth.

Daddy's influence of discipline in my life lives on in my own children as they now experience the "reap what you sow" principle.

> *Do not become dismayed at the baby steps and the small beginnings of each day.*

In fact, even this week I listened to one of my sons speak of the amazing garden he will have this spring and summer. He is committed to working in his garden several extra hours a week so it will produce abundance. Daddy loved to garden. I am also observing in my other son the discipline required to work on his master's degree online, which requires time every week so he can reap the benefits of this additional degree for more open doors for his family. Thank You, Jesus!

My advice to others and to myself: Do not become dismayed at the baby steps and the small beginnings of each day. Trust God's perfect timing for each stage of your growth as a creative. Let God be your source of strength and hope on this journey of small beginnings. Actively pursue the daily truth of our identity as a child of God made in His image. God is the giver of self-control. It is a fruit of the Holy Spirit given freely to God's children. Activate self-control to create the rhythms of discipline needed each day to reap the harvest and bring glory to God.

Reflections and Action Steps

- Reflect on a success in your past where you had the discipline to complete the task at hand. Celebrate your success.

- Think about a new area in your life where discipline can benefit your current situation. Can you take a step forward in discipline for five days? Ten days? Twenty days? Fifty days? One hundred days? Can you imagine your success of the completed goal?

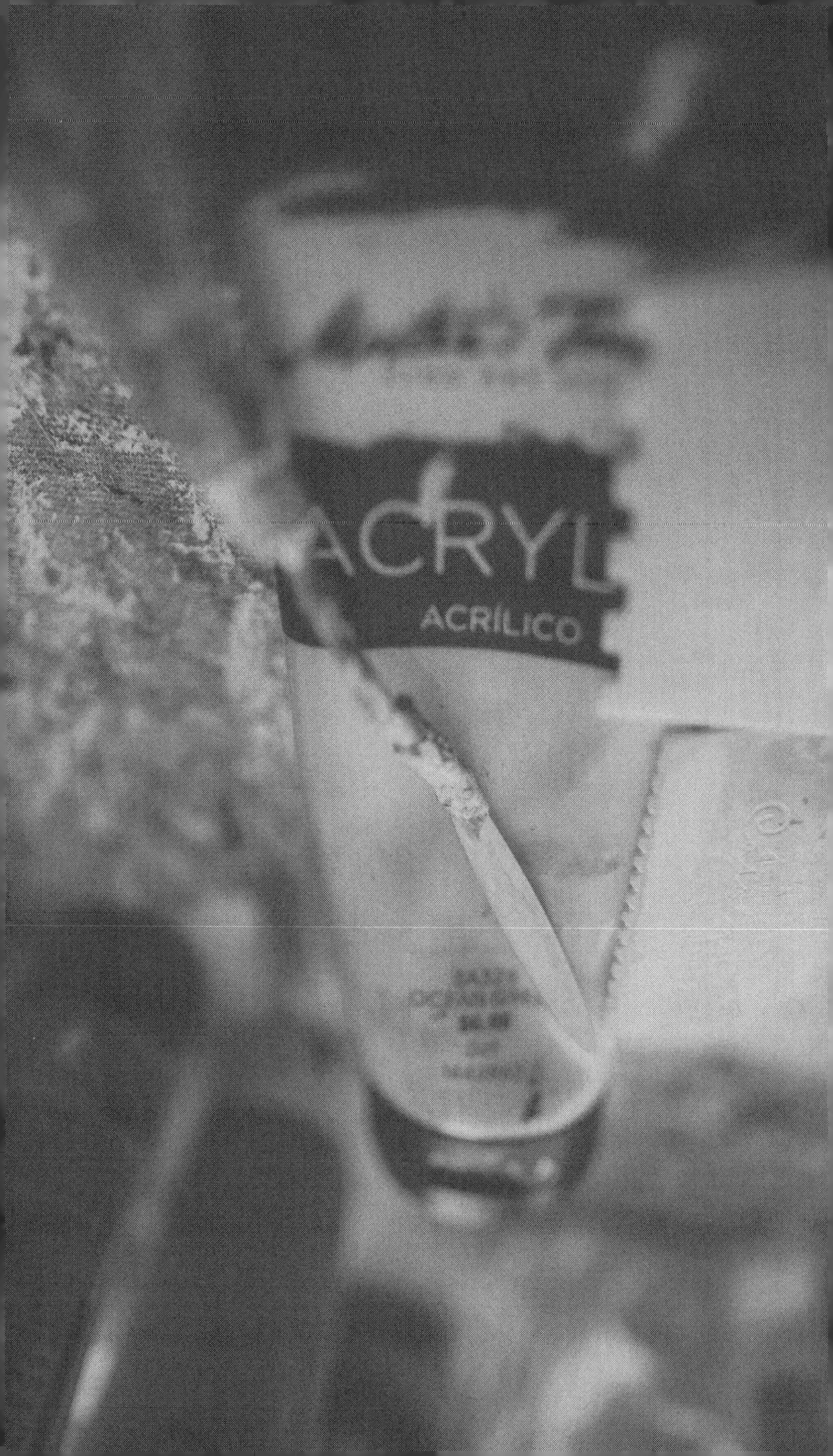
ACRYL
ACRÍLICO

chapter four

We need each other on this journey.

Find Your People

On my journey as an emerging artist, God has allowed me to be in different communities where I have learned to flourish. God knows how to create safe places and spaces for us to grow. Feeling emotionally safe is critical for my creative juices to flow. A community where one is not judged or compared to others is vital for growth. That is what creates the feeling of safety, getting rid of comparison so we can feel free to be uniquely ourselves. God made me and you in His image, the Creator's image. It is critical to find the people who believe the same is true so you all can thrive as artists.

My first creative team of people included the original group of women in my Cultivate gathering in October 2014. Lauren, Julie, Judy, Tracy, Amber, Holly, Tamia, Sondra, Lesa, Taylor. Each offered a unique perspective. Each a member of my first art community. Even after four years, these women are still speaking life into my art and love into my life.

From this first community of women who walked with me through my struggles, many still continue to speak words of encouragement to my journey of becoming an artist. They are my people. They are honest. They are real. They are true. Find your people. Nurture those relationships. This journey was not meant to be a road traveled alone.

The Rejection Card

"I am not an artist. Again, I am rejected from the juried art show. I don't think my paintings are any good." All I can hear is the negative chatter in my brain. This is me. I call my soul mate, Ann Younger, and dump my negative thoughts through the phone line. She encourages me to not give up. To get back up and try again. I ask her for suggestions and she gently

This journey was not meant to be a road traveled alone.

encourages me to move from a great place towards even more excellence in my work. She wears truth around her waist and brings out the best in me and my art.

I remember painting a heart on a 16x20 canvas using all of my extra paint from some other paintings my studio. I used many bright colors, but I did not know what strokes or color to add to make it stand out or give it definition. Ann told me what she observed as design elements in my artwork. I was unaware I used any of these elements, but Ann brought them into the light as part of my style.

> She said, *"Sara, on almost of all of your paintings you use an outline technique with uneven strokes created with wooden skewer sticks. Try outlining the figure with a darker paint and see what happens."*

Some months before, Ann introduced me to the skewer sticks as a fundamental painting instrument. In fact, she gifted me with my first five sticks in my painting tool repertoire. So, I tried using a raw umber (dark brown) color on the stick and rolled it over the surface of my painting in the outline of a heart. Oh, I loved it so much. The painting transformed from being passable to being a piece of art I loved. By Ann coaching me in this one small technique, it helped take my paintings to another level of excellence. Also, Ann advised attaching a paper backing to my giclee prints to increase the quality instead of just leaving them open like they come from the printer. My people make me better. Ann has helped me hone my skill set over and over again.

Another art community I joined in March 2018 is online with Matt Tommey. [18] When I found the group he leads on social media, I thought Matt was reading my mail. He mentors through his online group called Created to Thrive with training modules teaching others to thrive as artists. I attended the Gathering of Artisans in October 2018 and found more of my people. We worshiped the Creator, took classes and learned from each other. Each week we connect through social media, and my ability to feel part of this community has continually grown. We learn from one other and encourage and support each other all over the world as artists.

My latest art community formed with my home church, Bethel Austin, which opened its doors in September 2018. The Prophetic Art Team is

---

[18] matttommeymentoring.com

released to paint on the stage as part of our weekly worship services, and our artists have been well received by our church community. People express to me that they feel God's love through my paintings. Talk about humbling. Just a year ago I would have been terrified to paint in front of a worshiping congregation alongside other talented artists. Now I get to participate in this manner of worshiping our Creator.

God is stretching me to trust Him even more during the prophetic art worship time. During the first few months, God would let me know what I needed to paint before I went on stage. However, more recently, He waits until I am on stage. I think this is to teach me to listen and create with Him in the moment. It does not matter how many people are watching me. My prayer is that what I paint and how I paint will connect the hearts of those worshiping to His own heart.

DJ, a young man who watched me paint during worship recently, heard God speak into His life about how Jesus would never leave him. DJ had a vision that he was inside of my painting. He saw himself in the painting with Jesus by his side.

At the end of worship, I was talking with a woman who had never seen painting in the midst of corporate worship. As we discussed this, DJ came bolting up to talk with me about the painting. He wanted to know if he could buy it and asked how much it was. I told him the price, it was over $500. He told me he couldn't pay that amount. The woman I was talking with, someone neither of us had met, told me that she would be right back. She showed back up with a credit card in hand. She bought the painting for DJ.

People helping people. What generosity! Sometimes God calls me to give my paintings away, but this time He blessed DJ through the gift of a stranger.

DJ has a call on his life to be a missionary overseas. The name of the painting is *"His Light Will Be Seen."* The light of Jesus will be seen because of the obedience of DJ. And I am honored to be another person in DJ's corner.

Safety in Creativity

When I began painting in the Cultivate group, I laughed at God and said, *"No way! I am like an 18 month-old. I have no idea what I am doing!"* This continual negative thread of thoughts flowed through my head on most Tuesday mornings. Intimated by the blank canvas. I was afraid ideas or images could not or would not come into my mind. I prayed and asked God for something before I came to the session so I could feel safer. Feeling safe in the midst of new and vulnerable experiences seemed to be a tightrope walk. Would I fall off the rope into fear and immobility, or take a step forward on the rope?

Many times He had me wait until I was in class to show me what He wanted on the canvas that day. It was a training ground of listening to God, to hear Him in my thoughts and learning to recognize the still quiet voice of my Creator. It was not audible, but they were clear, new thoughts that were different from the old record player of my own nega-

Pictured: "His Light Will Be Seen"

tive thoughts. Trust Him in the painting. Trust Him in the process. Trust Him in the outcome. Just simply trusting God Almighty, my Creator, was creating something new in me. He was making me a new creation by taking away, layer by layer, the old creation full of lies and unbelief. Take a deep breath and pick up the paintbrush. Do not be afraid—fear will rob you of the joy of creating.

In our circle time, we shared our thought processes in hearing God during quiet times of painting, and there was no dialogue with others the rest of the time. There was only dialogue with God. This helped to facilitate open ears and eyes to what God's voice sounded like to me. Determined to have God win this battle of the emerging artist within me, I wanted His voice to be louder than the voice of defeat. Over these six weeks, I learned to discern truth over the lies. This began my journey toward hearing God for the next layer, both on and off the canvas.

One particular Tuesday morning, after four weeks of Cultivate, an "outsider" walked into the room where we were painting. I felt relatively safe before this particular day. I usually set up my painting space outdoors on the patio, but this day I set up inside. I can still feel the total shutdown. I did not feel safe. I felt totally vulnerable and blocked. My creativity was closed off immediately and I walked away.

Reflecting on this experience has helped me to overcome similar circumstances. What factors influenced my shutdown? God helped me understand what happened. The major factor that influenced my inability to paint in front of others was a looming fear of failure. My performance was on the line. Being judged and not knowing how others would react to my painting lead to a creative block.

In time, God's love overtook my fears and turned painting into an active choice of faith. Getting back in front of others to paint and facing my fear of failure head-on did not happen overnight. I had to continually choose to believe that I was who God said I was. I had to remember my purpose was not to serve man but to serve God. I had to keep my eyes set on the knowledge that honing my craft would take time, energy and discipline. I cannot despise these small things, these little steps of movement that got me where I wanted to be, able to walk the tightrope fearlessly, balanced and upright.

I have come a long way, baby! Move forward a few years and now I paint in public with great joy and unrestrained creativity. This is a huge change, which I could never have imagined previously. This first six weeks of discovering that I am an artist was the beginning of me believing what God told me. *"I am an artist for God."* This changed the course of my life.

Over the next few months, I continued to participate in Cultivate experiences, even as a facilitator. I helped to guide other "non-artists" and "artists" on the journey of creativity, with God as the teacher. I continued to let my mind be transformed. I chose to believe the truth that I had the creative DNA from Jesus. He is the Great Creator and I am made in His image. So, therefore, I too am a creator made to create to bring glory to God. Engaging in the process of creating art while hanging out with God allows His thoughts to become my thoughts.

In July 2016 I took one of my intuitive acrylic pieces over to a dear friend's house. I asked her to pray over my art and ask God for the next steps with me. The title of this piece—"In The Garden" found its home. Julie fell in love with the piece and wanted to buy it from me. I never expected her to buy the piece of art. She knew about our upcoming mission trip to Mongolia for several months and this money would help our travel fund. Had I just sold my first piece of acrylic art? Did this make me an artist for God? Someone would pay money for what I had painted? I was in shock and truly grateful. I felt something new had started for me. But I really had no idea what would happen next. How good can God be? I so wanted to call my Mama and tell her what had just happened. But I knew she knew. She was cheering me on in the "huge cloud of witnesses" [19] Her daughter just sold a piece of artwork.

The Tapestry of the First Painted Angel

How my first angel painting ended up with God's purpose

Our time in Mongolia was challenging due to harsh weather conditions and big changes in our diet and routines. In mid-September 2016, I wrote my "impossible prayer". Of course, I did not know at the time I wrote that prayer when God would answer, but I kept painting.

Our kids were taking language classes, so they were not home during the day. Wayman and I stayed in the apartment most days and ventured out to buy groceries and go to some markets. I bought extra canvases and found myself painting almost every day in the apartment. I loved giving the paintings away to those serving and to some of the local Believers who participated in Worship and Art Nights.

---

[19] Hebrews 12:1 NLT

Then one day I started painting a group of angels on the canvas. I think there were eight angels in the painting. I was inspired by the artist I follow on Instagram, Deanne Herbert. It was painted on a 20x24 canvas. My very first angel painting. I loved this painting. The name was *"Heavenly Hosts."* I knew I would not bring it back to Texas with me, but I had not heard who I was to give it to. I asked my daughter-in-love, Rachel if she knew who I was to give it to. She said, *"I want it!"* Thrilled, I gave it to her. She and Samuel would be moving to their new country in Central Asia in a few months and she could take this piece with them.

In their last week in their apartment in Ulaanbaatar, Mongolia, they invited a brother and sister from Western Mongolia who were not yet Believers over for dinner. These young people were from the same country that Samuel and Rachel were about to move to in Central Asia. Sunny, the young woman, saw the angel painting leaning against the wall of the hallway and asked Rachel about it. She loved it. Rachel asked if she wanted it as a gift, and she did! Only God could write this story. My very first angel painting is in Mongolia, in the apartment of a young woman and her brother. I still pray they have said "Yes" to Jesus at this point in time. I might not ever find out. But I do know that God strategically placed my first angel painting in the hands of a non-believer.

"Do Not Fear" Mighty Man of God

A testimony of one man's heart connection to my art

While painting in Fredericksburg I looked up to see a man wearing a black National Guard t-shirt staring at my paintings on the sidewalk. He listened quietly to my story of becoming an artist. I asked him if he wanted to sign up for my monthly newsletter. He declined. I told him I respected his decision. Then he said, *"I am so moved by your paintings. I really don't even have words. There is something here, I can feel it. I can't even speak."*

This man was sensing the working of the Holy Spirit. To hear another speak of the power of the Holy Spirit anointing that is on these paintings was powerful to me. Strength and confirmation that God's blessings are on this art.

In that moment I wondered if I was worthy to carry the anointing of painting for Him.

"*Yes!*" He told me, "*Just keep giving Me all the glory.*"

And then I heard the recognizable whisper of my Father, "*Give him a painting.*"

I said to the man, "*Can you wait here a minute? I have something for you.*"

I stepped quickly inside the store and find a strong mighty angel named, "*Do Not Fear*", and I knew this was the one. This angel carried a message of a strong and mighty man full of valor for the Lord. God knew this moment would happen when I had painted "Do Not Fear Angel" about two weeks previously. He knew this angel in dark blue and gray tones would be this man's angel to symbolize God's unconditional love for him. God wrote this story.

I brought him the angel named "Do Not Fear", and he accepted the gift.

I asked him, "*Can I pray for you?*"

He said, "*Yes.*"

When I closed my eyes and began praying I saw the Angel of the Lord coming to Gideon. I began saying words of hope and strength and bravery

Pictured: "Do Not Fear"

over this man in the prayer. I told him that the LORD sees him and has such wonderful plans for him. The pain and mistakes were wiped clean. God has such a destiny for him to be a mighty man of the LORD, for his family and his future. After praying he looked at me, wiping tears from his eyes. He asked if he could give me a hug. I gave him permission and I whispered God's strong love over him and told him that he is not alone.

He said, *"Thank you!"* and went on his way.

And I said to God, *"Thank You for this holy intersection of power and love."*

At first, it seemed as if this man was not interested in my art when he declined to join my email list. And then, with a little time, God used our encounter to show His love.

Not only do I charge you with the task of finding your people and surrounding yourself with them, but you should also go find others that you can support. You need to be a cheerleader for others. Encourage, encounter and speak truth into those around you. Be to others what you are also needing. Keep pouring out what He has given you and God will fill your cup to overflowing. Again. And again.

Walking this path as an artist alone would be more arduous and difficult without my people. God built us for relationships. He sends us cheerleaders and coaches along the way. Family and friends are meant to be positive influences in our journey. My tribe helped me find and take the next step. I am forever grateful for each interaction from others that spurred me onward. God continues to help me on my journey of more small beginnings, meeting others and adding to my tribe.

Reflections and Action Steps

• Write a list of your people. The people you can call in the middle of the night for difficult situations. The tribe who dances with you in those joyous celebrations.

• Now ask God to add to your tribe. Ask Him to show you the one in your community, your family, your social network who needs your care and attention. Reach beyond your own tent. Move out your tent stakes. Watch what God will do with your actions of love.

chapter
five

God is up to something in the detours.

Walk Out On The Water

My thoughts would see-saw back and forth every eight weeks at the local juried art show hosted by our local art league:

> *"Here I go again. I have to go up to bat or I will never hit a home run. They are not going to take my paintings. I keep putting out money and don't get a return on my investment. I hate going back in the afternoon at the designated time to walk the hall of shame and see that all four of my entered paintings, yet again, have been "rejected" and "unchosen." Again. And again.*
>
> *Maybe I should go at the beginning of the hour to pick up my paintings. Will I feel less rejected? Because I had been going at the end of the hour to pick up and there were my paintings among only a few still unclaimed rejections. Mine were leaning against the wall like wilting flowers."*

So next time, I went at the beginning of the hour to pick up my rejections. I can tell you, the pain was not lessened regardless of the timing.

My inner dialogue continued, *"Why do I put myself through this?"*

It was painful. The woman who works behind the desk would help me find my "rejects", and said once, *"Just keep trying. The artwork was so good this time. The juror had such a hard time deciding and we only have room for so many."*

And I admit, I asked My Man many times to go pick them up for me and call me with the rejection notice. It seemed to soften the blow a bit coming from the one who has stood by my side for more than 30 years. I always seemed to be busy on those particular days. Wayman was faithful to go, but I realized this was my responsibility to go up to bat. I had to put on my big girl underwear and go to see if they had a place to hang on the walls as watchmen.

Choosing to believe who God says you are is scary. Why do we feel so exposed? When I read about the Hall of Fame of the Faithful in Hebrews 11, I see men and women who risked everything to serve their Abba Father. I dreamt of serving Him in such a way. And yet, when He told me exactly what to do, it took years for me to believe Him.

Think back to a moment in a little fishermen's boat in the Sea of Galilee. Peter, a disciple of Jesus, looked out on the water in the middle of the night. He and the other disciples saw something coming. It looked like a ghost. Then he recognized the face. Jesus, a man they had just seen feed thousands of people with just a few loaves of bread and a few fish, is walking on the water across the Sea of Galilee to come and find them.

Walking on the water.

He doesn't believe it. He wants Jesus to prove it is Him. And then, Peter gets an invitation.

"Come," Jesus said. So Peter gets out of the boat and begins to walk toward Jesus. Once Peter is out on on the water, he gets distracted.

> "But when he saw the wind, he was afraid and, beginning to sink, cried out, "Lord, save me!" Immediately Jesus reached out his hand and caught him. "You of little faith," He said, "why did you doubt?" And when they climbed into the boat, the wind died down. Then those who were in the boat worshiped Him, saying, "Truly you are the Son of God." [20]

Peter experienced something that I fought for so long, a battle of the mind. Who are you going to believe? What is the worst that will happen? Get out of the boat, and if you start to sink, Jesus will catch you.

The struggle is real. I certainly do not have all the answers. But I share with you my mind battles. I go back to the truth of who I am. I am a Child of God. I am made in the Creator God's image. In His likeness. He creates, so I create. It is what I am meant to do. To be. To become. To process.

---

[20] Matthew 14:30 NIV

All the doubts and lies, they are like fiery arrows trying to find their way under my skin.

To live every day. But I trust the dreams God placed in my heart to move to reality, and I believe in a new identity. Walking out on the water.

All the doubts and lies, they are like fiery arrows trying to find their way under my skin. When these darts find their way to where they were intended to be, they shut me down. They distract me. They get me off track. They are not new or creative. Some days they are there, some days they aren't. And they are the same ones I struggled with from the very beginning.

> *There is no way I am an artist.*
> *I don't know what I am doing.*
> *I have no formal training, so I am really not an artist.*
> *The professional juror at the art show can see right through my amateur status. They just keep passing over me. Why do I even try to get into an art show? It is a waste of money.*
> *I will never be able to paint like her.*
> *I can't learn how to do art software programs to produce other art products to sell.*
> *This is too much for me.*
> *I am so afraid it is crippling.*
> *I am painting and not hanging out with my friends.*
> *This is so lonely.*
> *What is the next step in growing my business?*
> *How do I get customers beyond my friends?*
> *What do I paint next?*
> *I don't know how to paint that.*
> *I wish people would stop telling me what to paint!*
> *Do they know I don't really know what I am doing?*

The comparisons and the lies. They grew like a wet psyllium.

But there is more to it. Peter has enough faith to step out of the boat. After he is ALREADY WALKING ON WATER, he doubts. He seems to have a hard time. There is a real obstacle of the water sloshing around him, as well as the gripping fear. It doesn't go away once he steps out of the boat. With each step he still had fear.

As with any life pathway, obstacles are going to show up. Some are expected and some are a surprise. Am I going to let fear stifle my dreams or passion when the hard places and hard times appear? Sometimes one wins with decisions made on the journey. And sometimes one loses with decisions made on the journey. But, really, did I lose or did I just learn from my decisions? It all depends on the perspective I choose to believe. When I start to sink, I feel Jesus grab me, hold me tight, and tell me not to lose faith. I hear His whisper saying, "Take another step. I am with you."

The Vision of Psalm 91

I hear His whisper saying, "Take another step. I am with you."

A story of how God showed me the reality of angels in the midst of a trial

Psalm 91 is a scripture that makes an appearance quite often. In May 2012 this scripture took on a new meaning for me. For two years I had been the principal of a middle school in central Texas. Without going into too many details, my time at this school was filled with intensity and stress. I asked a friend for prayer one afternoon after a particularly difficult meeting. She asked God to give me both a vision and a clear explanation for that vision. This was new territory for me. I had never had a vision before. Simply asking for a vision felt like stepping out on the water. It felt like a risk. What if we ask this bold prayer and He doesn't speak to me?

That very night I had a vision where I wore a white dress that came to my knees and angels held me high off the ground. When I looked down, I saw hundreds of gray and black snakes writhing below me. This was particularly intense for me because I hate snakes. But they couldn't reach me. The angels were holding me high above them. I wasn't sure what it meant until I told this vision to my son, Justin. He immediately knew and said,

"Mom, read Psalms 91!".

> *"For He will order His angels*
> *to protect you wherever you go.*
> *They will hold you up with their hands*
> *so you won't even hurt your foot on a stone.*
> *You will trample upon lions and cobras;*
> *you will crush fierce lions and serpents under your feet!*

The Lord says, "I will rescue those who love Me.
I will protect those who trust in My name.
When they call on Me, I will answer;
I will be with them in trouble.
I will rescue and honor them.
I will reward them with a long life
and give them My salvation." [21]

I couldn't have made that up. It was too perfect. We have a Living God. We have a God who speaks to us. We have a God that we can trust, that we can risk for, that we can walk toward even if it seems impossible, improbably, or intimidating. Through this experience, I began to put a foot out onto the water. We were bold in our prayer and He was bold in His response.

A Final Miracle in Ulaanbaatar

A testimony to help my unbelief

Our time with our children in Mongolia in 2016 was so special. We fell in love with these strong, brave and obedient young Believers we were spending time with. But traveling smart in some countries requires new eyes and ears. It is not my quiet little Texas town. It is not always rainbows and butterflies. We needed some practical instruction on how to be safe. Within the first day of our arrival, our son gave us very specific instructions on how to protect our personal belongings. Specifically, he told us how to protect billfolds and cell phones while out of the apartment. Many of the young Mongolians on the street were unemployed and thievery is a way of life. They are expert pickpockets. This was extremely prevalent on the buses, at bus stops, in the markets and on crowded sidewalks. Samuel went over the exact steps to take so that we could avoid being victims. He had reported to us that in every American service group that came, at least one (and usually several) lost their phones and/or money. He did not want us to fall into that category.

About four days before departing from Mongolia, we all went to the big market in Ulaanbaatar. It was very crowded along the sidewalks. I walked ahead with one of the young Mongolian girls while Wayman walked behind with Samuel and Rachel. The girl and I stopped to let them catch up, and we saw Samuel coming urgently toward us with a very intense look on his face. He said, *"Dad got pickpocketed!"* Samuel was so mad and he was walking quickly trying to find the thief.

---

[21] Psalms 91:11-16 NLT

Then Wayman walked up and explained he had been jostled between two young men. When Rachel looked at Wayman's upper coat pocket she could see that it was unzipped. She said, *"Check your pocket"* and Wayman's billfold was gone. In that very moment Rachel said, *"Jesus, I ask for the billfold to be returned immediately."* We all stood in a tight circle talking when I saw a hand appear from nowhere with Wayman's billfold. The young thief brought back the billfold and handed it to Wayman as we were standing in the circle. The theif said in Mongolian, *"Take care of this!"* Then he quickly walked away from us.

Wayman checked his billfold and all money and credit cards were there. Nothing was missing! This happened within two or three minutes after it was stolen. As we stood together on the edge of the market in a circle, we knew God had heard Rachel's prayer. What more could we do besides praise and thank the God of Angel Armies?

Our Mongolian friend said she had never heard of a thief returning any stolen propert. We had just witnessed a miracle. Rachel had called out to Jesus for help. Jesus immediately changed the young thief's heart. We pray for this young man and believe we will see him in heaven. Who knows why he decided to hand Wayman back his billfold? Maybe he had an encounter with Holy Spirit, or Jesus Himself. Wouldn't that be amazing? Whatever it was, it must have been a radical encounter

Pictured: Wayman, Rachel, Sara and their Mongolian friend*

for the young man who took it. I don't even want to call him a "thief". Maybe that experience changed the course of his life. We will find out in heaven.

When I think back to that experience, I see another example of how God responded to our bold prayer. When we ask with a spirit of expectancy, not expectation or as an order, He will show up. That is not to say He will always do exactly as we ask, no. We must have expectancy and not expectations. Expectancy means we know we can trust our good God and what He is doing. Expectation means we think He will do it our way. But, because of the work that Jesus did on the cross, we can ask. Our God loves to surprise us with His love when we have stepped out of the boat.

Moving from Cultivate to Selling

Another small beginning

Several 100 Day Projects with art from April 2015 to the spring of 2016 kept my mind and hands working on my artistic skills. None of my acrylic paintings were sellable. In fact, a friend told me recently that when she saw my artwork in the spring of 2016 she was surprised I even painted. I obviously had self-awareness about the quality of my work; however, the marriage between my daily art practice and my time of worship with Jesus was a holy intersection. I felt His presence and heard His voice in the midst of creating in my daily discipline. This time of intimacy with God was driving my creativity and moving me into a beautiful relationship. My soul was singing, so I tried to not let my insecurity keep me from creating. Perfectionism steals the joy in the journey of creating. Seek to understand the process towards excellence with each step.

I continued to help facilitate the Cultivate sessions at our local church for several semesters. His holy unveiling brought my fellow worshipers and painters to the throne room during those sessions. I became more comfortable with each ongoing session and saw God use the process of creating art to show His love for His children in new ways.

On January 1, 2016, I knew I needed to start another 100 Day Challenge. I decided to paint with watercolor every day, and, again, connect each piece to scripture. It started out great for the first 60 days or so, and then I waned in the journal entries. A transition occurred. I started to actually create product in the form of watercolor note cards to sell.

And since I was selling my notecards, I stopped my art journal entries. I sold them for about five dollars a card. But yet, I still did not really believe I was an artist.

The Impossible Dream at Home

Over Christmas vacation, soon after selling my first painting the month before, we were out at my stepson's property in the Texas Hill Country for about a week. Still so new in this journey of selling my artwork, I couldn't stop painting in my free time. I used the outside deck as my studio. It had been about 14 weeks since my prayer of the impossible in Mongolia. God was about to surprise me even more with His impossible plans.

On the evening of December 26, 2016, I got my first commissioned piece, a 30x30 from a dear friend and former co-worker. She contacted me through social media. This was affirmation, but I was full of fear. I had not painted anything bigger than 12x12. Could I paint something big and the finished product be worth selling? I was in shock, but I knew God continued to answer my impossible prayer. Little by little, step by step, God opened doors that no man could open.

I felt the anointing from God come in a way that had not been there before. Painting angels became my focal point. My process of painting included reading scriptures about angels daily and asking God for revelation before I began to paint. Psalm 91 had always been Mama's favorite passage of scripture, but now it became a near daily mediation for me. Not only was it part of my first vision from God, but now it inspired my art years later.

Pictured: Sara's Angel note cards

"Those who live in the shelter of the Most High will find
rest in the shadow of the Almighty.
This I declare about the Lord: He alone is my refuge, my
place of safety;
He is my God, and I trust Him.
For He will rescue you from every trap
and protect you from deadly disease.
He will cover you with His feathers.
He will shelter you with His wings.
His faithful promises are your armor and protection.
Do not be afraid of the terrors of the night,
nor the arrow that flies in the day.
Do not dread the disease that stalks in darkness,
nor the disaster that strikes at midday.
Though a thousand fall at your side,
Though ten thousand are dying around you,
these evils will not touch you.
Just open your eyes,
and see how the wicked are punished.
If you make the Lord your refuge,
if you make the Most High your shelter,
no evil will conquer you;
no plague will come near your home.
For He will order His angels
to protect you wherever you go.
They will hold you up with their hands
so you won't even hurt your foot on a stone.
You will trample upon lions and cobras;
You will crush fierce lions and serpents under
your feet!

The Lord says, "I will rescue those who love Me.
I will protect those who trust in My name.
When they call on Me, I will answer;
I will be with them in trouble.
I will rescue and honor them.
I will reward them with a long life
and give them My salvation." [22]

---

[22] Psalms 91 NLT

Acts 1:8 Blessings Business Beginnings

These are the steps we took on this journey of starting a small business. We suggest that you glean your own information for your specific state or country from accountants and attorneys. We are not in any way advising your steps, just sharing our process of those first years.

On November 7, 2016, I posted on my personal FaceBook page a picture of an 8x8 angel I had painted. That day I sold my first acrylic angel painting! This was a small beginning. I had no idea that over the first two years of my art business I would sell over 750 paintings and gross over $55,000 in art sales. This first painting sold for $32.

God does not intend for us to be starving artists. I have increased the selling price of my art gradually. I found the sweet spot where my paintings were selling and slowly increased the prices. God wants us to be blessed. He wants us to be provided for. As believers, we need to have a heart of service and provision for others, but that does not always look the same for each person. Jesus told some to drop everything and follow Him. But He also told some to stay in their sphere of influence. Selling ourselves short because we think we are supposed to does not bring glory to Him. Listening to His voice and responding in obedience does. Selling my art for what it is worth blesses me and then I use my blessing to bless others. I claim His goodness over all God's artists. Our work carries His kingdom, and it should bring provision along with the light and love of Jesus.

Selling ourselves short because we think we are supposed to does not bring glory to Him.

In the last few weeks of December 2016, I felt a stirring in my spirit to provide funds for missions and others in need around the world. Wayman and I knew we needed to start a business. When Ann and I had done the fundraiser for Samuel and Rachel in October of 2014, Acts 1:8 was the purpose and heart behind our event. Ann painted the scripture on a large piece of old metal roofing tin that we used for decoration. This piece of metal is in the corner of my studio as a reminder of our God-ordained purpose. This was His business. God Himself leads the way in every place and in every step.

We were ready to take the business just one step further. That is really all this process has been, one step further in, then another, then another. That is how we found ourselves where we are today.

Starting a business can be overwhelming. We knew our most important task was to keep producing. For us, that was paintings. Each step was drenched in prayer as we listened to what God said. We didn't want to take our eyes off of Him. We met with our small business consultant, Abbey Henderson, on January 2, 2017. She gave us great advice about separating our financials, getting a DBA (Doing Business As) registered in our county courthouse.

We had enough money from sales in November and December 2016 that we did not need a small business loan to get started. We were able to open a separate bank account. For our state sales taxes, we kept a separate record of our sales in a free online program/application called Wave. We then registered through our state comptroller's office to get a tax ID set up. In Texas, currently, if we sell art out of state we are not required to pay the state sales tax.

Our federal taxes hit us pretty hard the first year, so now we are paying our federal estimated taxes quarterly out of our profits. We now have a certified public accountant doing our taxes for our business and it has taken a huge burden off our shoulders. Our accountant has advised us to become an LLC as we have expanded our sales over the first two years. Again, small beginnings that grow.

Our first printing job was for "Our Story" cards. These cards were used to tell our story and purpose behind Acts 1:8 Blessings. It has been wonderful to have these to hand out to customers and potential customers. Our purpose came before we even had business cards. We then had our business cards printed a few months later and use them even more frequently than our story cards since they are small and more economical.

We have a URL and website through a website builder called Squarespace. God helped us make a connection with a college senior pursuing a graphic art degree and we paid him to help us get started. We love

Pictured opposite: Sara's first acrylic angel painting

the company that we use as our website builder and can manipulate our data and redesign pages as we see the need without having to pay others. It has an online store within the website. We also started business pages on two forms of social media, FaceBook and Instagram.

Then I started an Etsy store. I spent hours learning how to do tags and set up my items to sell by watching videos. I had one sale off of Etsy and then turned off my store. After that sale, I realized that my goal is to sell from my own website and drive business there instead of through another website.

The Etsy shop was a lesson in looking for the long lasting-fruit. Look for the long-lasting fruit and spend your time harvesting there. It doesn't mean you stop sowing seeds. Never stop. God wants us to go where the harvest is. Even though I turned off my Etsy storefront, I am still using things I learned in the process about online sales and internet marketing.

The way we are doing our business is not the only right way or the best way. It is just the way we are doing it. What is next, God? Show us! What we hear from Him is the next step in the right direction. If we fail, then we learn from our mistakes and wait for the next direction. We will keep taking the next step.

"There's No Shadow You Won't Light Up"

A story of a father hearing God clearly

I waited for a parking space right in front of the store with my flashers on because I saw taillights light up. But then a couple got out of their pickup with the dogs to take them for a walk. I had wanted their parking space right in front of the boutique, but had to park elsewhere. Finding a parking space on Fredericksbrug's busy Main Street challenges my patience.

I noticed when the couple came back to their pickup, but a customer had my attention. I decided to stay and do what I was doing instead of running down the street to get my car and move it to their parking spot. I knew I would have to move my car closer later in the day to load up my paints, easel, and the rest of my accoutrements.

Earlier in the day, while I pulled out my art supplies and paintings to set up on the sidewalk, I asked God which paintings I needed to show on the outside ledges and bench. He answered me. I took out an origi-

nal bright cactus painting on wood that had been tucked away on one of the inside shelves of the shop. Wayman had cut the wood for me and framed it. It was an 8x9 and I had named it after a line from Cory Asbury song called *"Reckless Love"*. The line was "There's No Shadow You Won't Light Up," and the painting with the same name sat on the bench in front of the store.

After the man had loaded up his dogs and gotten in his pickup, he saw the painting. He got out and came over to the painting. Tears began to well up in his eyes. I walked up to him. His wife joined him and they shared the story of their once wayward teenage daughter. Earlier in the year, she ran away from home. They declared the words of this very song over her while she was gone. The daughter came back home, safe and sound, and soon after decided to follow Jesus.

All of that, paired with the fact that her favorite plants are cacti, filled them with emotion. "There is No Shadow You Won't Light Up" was meant to be for their daughter. You could see in their faces that they felt God's presence. He whispers to us *"I see you."* But that day, they heard it loud and clear. It was a trumpet sounding. I prayed with them and thanked God for all He has done and will do through their daughter. This Dad was overwhelmed with God's love and tender touch. This special Christmas gift painting from father to daughter symbolized God's love and attention to detail in this story He is writing.

Pictured: "There's No Shadow You Won't Light Up" and new owners

Peter, The One Who Walked on Water

When Jesus called Simon Peter to be His follower, he had an interesting response. He said, *"Oh Lord, please leave me— I'm such a sinful man."* [24] Peter, the rock of the church. Peter, a man who risked his life time and time again to share the gospel. Peter, a man who was crucified upside down. His response when Jesus first called him was that he was too sinful to join. Isn't that our response sometimes? I can't do that, Jesus. It's too risky, I'm too sinful. If you only knew what I've done you would leave me here and move on to someone else.

Jesus doesn't see us for who we are in that moment, He sees us for who He created us to be. He calls out who we really are as we walk our lives with Him. Peter became "the rock" because he walked with Jesus. It takes practice; it takes trust. We can take risks because of what Jesus did, not because of what we have done. Based on our track record, we don't have the power. But look at Jesus' track record. He is so worthy. Step out of the boat and walk to His hand that is reaching out to you.

Eventually, the negative thoughts became few and far between. But when I get into new situations and I am stretched out of my comfort

Jesus is leading our dance.

zone, I begin to have doubts again. Most recently, this happened during an art show in Atlanta in January 2019. By the complete hand of God, I was invited to come to this art show, and I had high expectations. But those expectations were not met. In fact, it was quite difficult to be there. I felt like I began to doubt and then sink. That can happen when my expectations begin to outweigh the expectancy I have for God to move the way He wants to.

Sometimes doubts can come when I start tinkering with a new style of art, like my encaustic pieces, or when I have new subjects that I'm painting. I can move from a place of peace and then start the mental gymnastics all over again. I'm not sure this tension of walking on water to Jesus will ever stop. Be sure peace is your companion. If you lose peace, stop and turn to the Prince of Peace. He is waiting for you.

This journey began by taking small steps of faith. And, quite honestly, that has really never changed. It is still a discipline. Taking risks and trusting takes discipline and practice. Every day I have to believe all over again that I am an artist for God. I wish I could tell you that I never doubt anymore,

---

[24] Luke 5:8 NLT

that I have no trouble forgetting the waves around me and I continually keep my eyes on Jesus. But, I do. Still. Not every day. Not every week, but I do. It is all part of a journey— A journey of keeping my eyes on Jesus like Peter did, of believing that I can walk on water. My hand is in my Creator's hand. Jesus is leading our dance. He is walking beside me, calming the storm enough to guide me to the next step. He is the Prince of Peace, and He beckons us to walk to Him. Once we get to Him, we have to learn to walk with Him.

Reflections and Action Steps

• Reflect on the risks you've taken in your life. Have you taken any? Did you sink? Do you feel Jesus reaching to pulling you up?

• What are you thinking about more—what you are afraid of or what you are dreaming of? Journal your thoughts.

• Practice saying affirmations based on Scripture out loud about who God says you are. Start believing the things that seem impossible.

chapter
six

God hasn't ever not been talking.

Keep Your Eyes Open

"Do you make garden angels?"

I received this email from Phoebe Rogers, a friend in Houston, in the spring of 2017.

"What are garden angels?" I responded.

"I have a kitchen window above my sink looking out at a plain wooden fence. I would like to look at one of your angels when I am washing my dishes," Phoebe replied.

By keeping my eyes open, God has given me new ideas for art and for the business time and time again. In this example of discovering Garden Angels, I was able to create an angel that could be displayed outside. It started with the simple email request from my friend, Phoebe, and ended with Wayman and me creating an angel painted on wood with appropriate protective products so it could hang outside.

Wayman and I had to troubleshoot ways to create a weatherproofed piece of artwork. Together we came up with a 12x24, as this size fits in narrow spaces. I loved painting on wood, so we decided on plywood as our base. Wayman cut and primed them in preparation for me to create unique acrylic angels. This took several days of layering and waiting for each layer to dry. I still work this way. I usually have between five and twenty pieces of artwork in the process at the same time in my studio. While one is drying I move on to the next.

Wayman would take the angels back to his workshop and frame them with rough cut cedar made from fence pieces. He often told me that I could paint the angels faster than he could frame them. For these angels

to become weather-proofed, we had to determine how to seal the garden angels for protection. In our research, we found a weatherproof clear coat spray that does not turn yellow. Wayman sprayed three coats on the front side and one coat on the back side.

We sold over fifty garden angels in our first year, which fit well in a little niche in the market that we weren't even aware of. Including a chain on the back for hanging, we priced them at $48. Over that year, however, we found out that our garden angles didn't survive in climates with heavy rainfall and humidity. Some eventually had to be moved indoors.

In each season of our business, we reevaluate our products and determine what we want to keep making and selling. We retired the garden angels after making them for about 15 months. One of the main reasons for their retirement was the danger of using so many chemicals to make them waterproof. When we found out that they weren't even holding up in some places, it was even more of a reason to stop. It was a labor-intensive sequence, but our time and effort was not all lost. We learned how to work more effectively as partners in this process. For the first thirty-two years of our marriage we had worked closely together within our family, but not in an entrepreneurial sense. God used this time to show us how to do that more effectively.

Pictured: "Garden Angels" displayed at market

Acts 1:8 Blessings gleans new ideas and refines products from messages around us. Sometimes those messages are direct, and sometimes they are subtle. If I

It takes risk to follow what I feel like God is telling me to do.

don't keep my eyes open, I could easily miss them. The more we trudge down this road we are on, the more I realize just how intricately wrapped all of these lessons are. It takes discipline and practice to make sure my eyes and ears are open to what the Lord has for me. It takes risk to follow what I feel like God is telling me to do. It takes a constant reminder of why we are doing what we are doing so that I remember what it is all for. That is true not only in painting but also in business. All of it is braided together.

Recently we listened to a customer who asked us to put a more formal stained wooden frame on a garden angel, and we absolutely loved the look. So guess what? The original idea of a Garden Angel has now become a piece of fine art. The 12x24 acrylic on wood with a stained or painted wooden frame currently sells for more than three times the price of the original garden angel. New ideas and open doors often times have come from other people making suggestions for our business.

My Personal Art School Journey

I never took art classes in K-12 or college. Why would I? I was not an artist. But once God told me I was, I knew I needed a little training. There have now been three specific classes I have taken from professional artists. The first official training I had was a five-hour class in May 2015 with Suzanne King, a professional artist in the Austin area. We all painted

Pictured: Framed "Garden Angels"

a tree at sunset and practiced blending colors as we copied our instructor. Then, in the spring of 2016, I went to her open studio a few evenings. I practiced blending colors using a color wheel and had a mini-study on perspective in landscape. I completed an acrylic copy of Monet's "The Poppy Field" on a canvas panel over a period of about six weeks. This was a positive experience, but I was so unsure of my painting skills and considered myself still very amateur.

During a two-day intuitive acrylic painting workshop in late May 2016, I discovered more freedom in my painting style. Ann Younger and I planned an art retreat with worship as the center of our creative process. Annie Lockhart, a professional artist who leads similar workshops all over the country, lead nine women through prayer, intuitive painting and worship. Intuitive painting is a method of creative expression using color and paint with no intended outcome. I was very emotional during these two days. I had a huge battle going on in my mind. The gymnastics routine. It truly took so much of my energy to stay positive. My mind wanted to believe that I was never going to be any "good." Whatever "good" meant. A year and a half after I heard God whisper, *"You are an artist for Me,"* I was still in the battle of believing it was true.

Annie teaches with such freedom and hope for the canvas. She believes there are no mistakes. We paint in layers. Some of her key phrases were on repeat, and we needed to hear them:

> *"Don't get too fond of your current layer because likely the next layer will be better.*
>
> *Paint without fear. Use color. Use your hands. Use a sponge. Use a brush.*
>
> *If you don't like a certain area on your canvas, then paint over that area."*

There is not just one right way. Wait and see what emerges onto your canvas. Oh, and I discovered baby wipes. With a little gel medium and a baby wipe, you can take off some layers of acrylic paint and get to the underlying beauty. I now buy baby wipes by the case. They are my saving grace when I paint.

This workshop helped me find freedom and hope that I had yet to experience on the canvas. It was a turning point for me because I felt that I could be brave. My fear began to dissipate. I knew I could go back and fix it by uncovering or covering with more paint. I also learned experientially to use my hands and fingers instead of a paint brush, especially in the final stages. I left feeling more hopeful, but not over the top with my two pieces of intuitive art. As a marker of my art journey, "Heaven's Gate" is hanging in our bedroom as a reminder of some of my first paintings.

From the spring of 2015 through the summer of 2016, my heart was yearning to find extra income to help us purchase our plane tickets and take care of our travel expenses to go see our children in Mongolia. I prayed this prayer many times, *"God, please provide the extra funds needed."* We knew this was the first trip of many because our children were called to more than a few years of living overseas. With our retirement income, we are able to pay our bills and take care of our monthly expenses. But we desired another income stream to help with our additional travels and to help others who were on the mission field. We decided to operate in God's economy versus what the world tells us.

Our first small door opened for us to sell our art products in March 2016. I begin selling my watercolor note cards in the local co-op Senior Citizens Shop in our small Texas town of Wimberley, as well as a few assemblage pieces. These were similar to what I learned to do the previous fall with Ann. Wayman made wooden birdhouses, bird feeders and wooden trays.

My "training" was more of a collection of artistic experiences that I had picked up over time. And now this storefront was, in a way, a test. What was going to sell? What were people interested in? We kept our eyes and ears open to make sure we could do two things: stick with what we were interested in creating and make product people wanted. There is a way to do both and we wanted to do both well. Slowly but surely, our pieces sold.

Pictured: Sara with wood and assemblage pieces

Natasha's Angel

A story of an angel only God could write during our time in Russia

While we were in Mongolia with our children we took a ten day trip into Siberia. We went to visit two churches that were planted by the same organization connected with Samuel and Rachel. American teams started these churches some 22 years previously. They are now thriving churches fiercely in love with Jesus. The local Believers opened their homes, their community and their place of worship for a leadership conference. This was a vibrant and alive group of Believers. We started worship parties in the evenings that would go way past midnight because of the contagious movement of the Holy Spirit. Just like many of these types of trips, we were the ones blessed.

While in the city of Irkutsk, Russia, I met a beautiful woman named Natasha. She was battling cancer. Rachel and I prayed over her for healing several times. Natasha spoke Russian. I spoke English. But we understood each other because of the spirit of God. At one of our dance worship parties, Natasha came over to me and laid her head on my chest and began praying for me. We had a sisterhood connection. From time to time, after returning to the states, I would see her activity on social media and we would make a point to respond to each other's posts.

In early March 2017 she wrote me a message in Russian, knowing that I would be able to translate the message. I have iTranslate on my phone, but I did not take the time to translate it into English. A few weeks later I learned from a friend that Natasha had passed into the arms of Jesus.

In April, we traveled to Central Asia for our second visit with our kids. When I arrived I finally translated her message, almost a month after I had received it. She had asked if I could paint an angel for her.

I was so upset and disappointed that I had not communicated back to her before she left this earth. As I grieved I knew I had to paint an angel in her memory. Natasha is now healed, in the very presence of God. I found comfort in knowing that was true, but I still had such sadness.

I went to a nearby art supply store in the city and bought a 20x24 canvas to paint an angel in honor of Natasha. I wanted to send it back to Natasha's best friend in Russia. This angel turned out so beautiful. I knew God had helped me paint her. In fact, I put a cross in the lower

left corner, which is now one of my trademarks as an artist. I took a picture of "Natasha's Angel" with my iPhone. When I returned back to Texas in May, I decided to have 12x12 giclee prints made of this painting. "Natasha's Angel" has a special light and glory coming off of her. Wayman framed the giclee prints, and we have now sold many. God continues to use Natasha's story to bring hope and peace to others.

Even though I didn't have my eyes open from the beginning, Jesus took this situation and made sure His restoration trumped my shortfalling. God's love and grace never run out. God does not waste any part of your journey. He is writing your story perfectly, using all the broken pieces to create beauty from the ashes.

A Holy Connection

A story of the first gifted angel

The first time I heard the whisper of God telling me to give away a painting was just a few weeks after I sold my first. When I say "whisper," I don't mean that I have heard the audible voice of God. Rather, my thoughts were flooded with new ideas that I knew were not my own. I had an inkling to bring my box of paintings to work. I felt like I needed to show my current collection of angels to a friend at the local high school where I was a substitute teacher. Donna had suffered, she needed hope and was at an in-between place in her faith. Some of the paintings were as small as 3x3 and as large as 12x12. I could read her response as Donna looked through my box of paintings. She chose one and lifted it out of the box to inspect it more carefully. I saw her move the painting to her chest like she was holding it in an embrace. At that moment I witnessed the Holy Spirit connect to a person through a work of art. Tears filled her

Pictured: "Natasha's Angel"

eyes. Then she asked *"How much?"*, but we were interrupted with the work from the day. We both needed to be other places.

He is speaking. Will I keep listening?

I heard in my spirit, *"Give away this painting. It is a gift. It is Christmas. Wrap it up and deliver it."* I was obedient. I wrote a card, wrapped up the angel and delivered it to her classroom.

Later, she shared these words with me; *"When I see your angel, I feel close to God. I look at her every morning. I love how she makes me feel."* Even more than two years after I gave her the angel, she carries God's love.

God showed me early on that my paintings were really His paintings. My assignment was to release them when He told me to with joy. Through this process, I have heard in my spirit to give many away. Through these gifts, I hope the recipients hear God whisper to them, *"I love you. I see you. You matter to Me. I have not forgotten you. I am here waiting."*

With almost every angel I have given away there has been a message along with it. God speaks, I listen and pass on His message. The purpose behind this endeavor has never been for me to gain prestige or recognition. It has been to partner with God to spread His Good News near and far. This could seem like a daunting task, but it is not because I know the One who speaks.

Time after time God has shown me His will. What to paint. How to change a detail in the business. Where to sell. Who to talk to. What to say. God is in charge of my eyes and ears. He is speaking. Will I keep listening? Open eyes lead to open ears. Then we can begin the adventure of following Him even more. It is like a treasure hunt.

Reflections and Action Steps

• Think about a time you heard God give you a direction in your life. Celebrate His voice in your life.

• Ask for more encounters with God's voice. Ask Him to speak into your life. Take note of the sacred experiences.

chapter
seven

God is never going to run out of creativity.

Stick With Your Passions

At one point during His life on earth, Jesus lost many followers. He said and did things that were counter-cultural, and many people didn't know how to respond to Him. They grumbled, they left. But His original twelve stayed.

> *At this point many of His disciples turned away and deserted Him. Then Jesus turned to the twelve and asked, "Are you also going to leave?"*
>
> *Simon Peter replied, "Lord, to whom would we go? You have the words that give eternal life. We believe and we know you are the Holy One of God."*[24]

When things get hard, it is our passion that keeps us moving forward. They could have left, they could have moved on, but they knew the truth. How could they pick anything else? Following Jesus was the only thing to do. There was no one else.

This journey has been hard. You already know about the mental gymnastics, the battle of choosing to believe that what God said was true is actually true. But past that, in the mundane, in the every day, and when things are complicated, I could have easily thrown in the towel. We are retired; we have the means to take care of ourselves. I don't have to do any of this. But I have passion. Really, I have so much more than that. I have true purpose, which feeds my passion.

This passion moves beyond the actual process of painting. When painting there are many physical layers to create the image, mood, and texture. The same is true in finding the passion for why we are walking

---

[24] John 6:66-69 NLT

down this path. The image is Jesus himself, the mood is a spirit of worship, and the texture is changed lives because of the art He is creating through me.

You have read the testimonies of lives changed throughout this book. Each testimony has a title and introduction, much like the introductions to each of the psalms. The stories themselves are a form of worship. The art is a form of worship, this book is a form of worship, all pointing to Christ and his power. There is no one else, it is only Him. Just like Peter, I have nowhere else to go and no one else to follow.

The Angel of Faith, Angel of Hope and Angel of Love

The story of the first set of note cards

You may remember that the first art pieces I sold in a storefront were handmade, individual note cards that were created from watercolor paintings I worked on during a 100 day challenge. The individual unique watercolor note cards were selling quite well, but I wanted to reproduce some of my art into printed note card sets.

It may seem like a simple idea, to take some of my original acrylic paintings and turn them into note cards, but the process was so overwhelming to me that it was only through passion and clear direction that I was even able to complete this task.

I have a tenacious "stick to it" type of personality. It has come in handy in this process. With each detail and with each step I asked God to lead. So many decisions. New territory. Which printer to use? Local or search for an online source? What size of notecards? How do I market the cards once I get them printed? What subjects do I turn into notecards? I asked Him. And with each day we got closer and closer to the final product.

Excellence has been a theme throughout this journey for me. Not perfection, excellence. I want to know that each art piece and business decision was made with excellence in mind. It is tedious to work this way, but the end result is always something that I am proud of, not something that I look at and think, *"that could have been better."*

Pursuing excellence leaves room for growth and honing a skill, while not expecting perfection.

Pursuing excellence leaves room for growth and honing a skill, while not expecting perfection. When I know I have worked on a project with as much care and effort that I am capable of, then I know I can be proud of the end result. I carried that into making these notecards. I wanted the writer of the note, as well as the receiver of the note, to notice the small details that make the card special.

In the beginning, I knew only a few details. I heard God's voice and He said over and over again—*"An Angel of Faith, Hope and Love. Paint them. Print them. Sell them."*

These three were foundational pieces, cornerstones for this new season of small beginnings. I was following the voice of my passion.

We planned a camping trip to one of our favorite places. Throughout the years we probably spent six Christmases camping in Big Bend National Park. It holds great memories and brings me a peace beyond understanding. Wayman and I decided to combine a camping trip with a painting trip to the Chisos Mountain Basin Campground in the park. I took seven 8x10 canvases to paint angels.

A week in the mountains to hike, to rest, to paint in the midst of serene beauty. I was so excited to have a bit of luxury, which included running water and a really comfortable bed in our travel trailer.

Every afternoon I would paint. Layers, color and texture. I completed seven paintings, but they remained unnamed. Which three would be the *"Angel of Faith"*, *"Angel of Hope"* and *"Angel of Love"*? I asked for input from some treasured friends and the names became clear. *"Angel of Faith"* was fair skinned with windblown dark hair dressed in a dark blue robe, ready to believe what she cannot yet see. Next, *"Angel of Hope"* was a medium skinned angel with a turquoise robe, ready to stand until

Pictured: Angel of Faith, Angel of Hope, Angel of Love

breakthrough comes. And lastly, the powerful *"Angel of Love"* was a dark skinned angel robed in cream and white, ready to love unconditionally.

You would think that the process of getting these angels onto the canvas would have been the hardest part; however, that was not the case. I did not know all the many steps still to come. If I would have known, I may not have agreed to the task. But I learned to stay the course, to follow through, and to stay passionate about the project in front of me.

The online notecard printing company I chose in Alabama required that I upload the images in a specific format with a software program I did not have or know how to use. In the midst of this ordering time, we were traveling overseas to Central Asia for a month to be with our kids. I was communicating with the company via email and several times by phone. Again, so much I did not know. It would have been so much easier to just say *"This is not working,"* and throw in the towel. But I heard the instruction from God that I could not let go of. I knew what needed to be done, and I kept moving forward.

I learned in this journey to trust when I hear God speak to me.

And finally, on Friday, May 5, 2017, delivered to my front doorstep were the Angel of Faith, Hope and Love notecards. I held them in my hands and I loved them! They arrived just in time for the outdoor garden club tour and art show that was taking place the very next day. More than three months of waiting came to an end.

Was it worth the effort, the tears, the persistence to bring these to completion? Yes, absolutely. I learned in this journey to trust when I hear God speak to me. None of this, the process of becoming an artist, the process of creating these note cards, any of it, would happen if it were not something I was passionate about. The purpose of wanting to serve, honor and please my Creator drives the burning passion to continue with a project until it is complete. What else is there? There is no one else.

I am not sure why these specific angels needed to be painted, printed and sold at this particular time. But God knows. There may have been one person, just one, who needed to have access to these cards. That makes it all worth it. He leaves the 99 to go and find the one. My true passion is to partner with Him in that process of finding that one person.

The Rabid Fox

My deep passion for angels and how my family and I were protected

I am sure we have all had them. We swerved at just the right time to miss a car accident. We trusted some gut feeling, made some decision, or were protected in some way. I don't think these things are accidents.

I notice them often now that I know what to look for, but my first true, tangible instance like this happened on Thanksgiving Day in 2000. We were out on my stepson's property enjoying time with our family. Our youngest son, Justin was eight years old. At about one o'clock in the afternoon, he and I decided to go out on the four-wheeler to check the perimeter fences while waiting for the turkey to finish cooking. We heard a loud pitched squealing sound and saw a fox attacking one of our dogs. I jumped off the four-wheeler to throw rocks and scare away the fox, but it came toward me. I lost my footing, slipped, and fell on the ground. The aggressive fox came and bit my right leg just below my knee. I was wearing capri pants, so my skin was exposed to the fox's bite. Justin was off the four-wheeler throwing rocks at the fox as well, and it ran behind a cedar bush. We quickly got back on the four-wheeler to drive back to the barn while the dog ran home in front of us. I knew that I had been bitten, but when I examined my leg back at the house my skin was fully intact. I was covered in blood and fox saliva, as well as some very faint red teeth marks, but I had no broken skin.

Wayman and our other sons went out immediately, in two separate vehicles, to find the fox. While they were looking, the fox started chasing them. My husband was able to kill it with his gun. We sent the fox's body to our state health department to test for rabies and it tested positive.

I had gone to the local hospital that day for treatment, but because of a mixup I didn't actually start my rabies treatment until four days later. There was no messing around once we knew the fox had tested positive for rabies. It is a fatal disease and enters the body through any open wound. I actually cut my knee a few days before Thanksgiving while shaving my legs. So, the fox did not tear my skin open, but I had an open wound due to my unskilled shaving abilities. It is funny today, but believe

There was something there that day shielding me from that fox.

me, on that particular day I was not laughing. It was not worth the risk, so I went through six consecutive weeks of rabies shots.

When I think back to this experience, to this day there is no other conclusion that I can come to besides that I was protected. My right leg should have been ripped to shreds, I should have been bitten a few times, I should have had more than just saliva all over my leg. There was something there that day shielding me from that fox. It was an angel. I still hold that experience as the beginning of my true belief in angels.

Painting Angels

I find it funny how many times people have asked me why I paint angels. I guess it happened so naturally in my worship that I didn't necessarily have a cognitive thought of "I know what I'll paint now, Angels!" It wasn't so intentional. But seeing and now understanding how angels have protected me throughout my life, I would say the most important reason I paint angels is because I know beyond a shadow of a doubt they were created by Almighty God. He instructs them to minister to the saints—*"Are they not all ministering spirits sent out to serve for the sake of those who are to inherit salvation?"* [26] He instructs them to be messengers of love—*"So bless the Lord, all His messengers of power, for you are His mighty hero who listen intently to the voice of His word to do it."* [27] He instructs them to sing praises to God for all of eternity *"All heaven will praise Your great wonders, Lord; myriads of angels will praise You for Your faithfulness."* [28] I am forever thankful to Jesus for the angels who have saved many lives and supernaturally protected my family, friends and all mankind. Another driving reason I paint angels is people like my paintings of angels. They sell. As an artist, if I am selling certain subjects, I am going to keep painting them. I also find so much joy in painting angels and I feel a deep sense of peace surround me as I paint them.

Our local high school art teacher, Donna, was the first person God told me to give a painting to. She is a dear friend and someone I respect as an artist and teacher. She told me early on in December 2016, about two weeks after I had sold my first angel painting, that she could see my style emerging and I should not change it. She said it was easy to distinguish my paintings and that unique style is what she tries to help her students find. Donna was so complimentary early on in my process that it helped me feel more confident in my distinctive style. This compliment carried me through times of doubt. When I was unsure, I remembered what

---

[26] Hebrews 1:14 NASB, [27] Psalm 103:20 TPT, [28] Psalm 89:5 NLT

Donna said. She is an artist, and she is a teacher. She knows what she is talking about. Her words carried weight. Donna is one of my people.

This is another question I get often— *"Why don't you paint faces on your angels?"* In fact, once when I was painting in Fredericksburg in the open doors of Loca on Main a Mom was shopping for clothes inside as a Dad was on "kid watch" outside. The six-year-old son was playing both inside and outside of the store. He could see my set-up and a good selection of my paintings. He was so intrigued and asked,

> *"Why don't you put faces on your angels?"*

> I laughed and said, *"I don't really know how to draw faces, so I just leave them without facial features, like eyes and a nose and a mouth."*

> He responded quickly, *"But you know how to draw bird's eyes!"* He had seen one of my painted buntings inside the store that has very distinct eyes.

> I replied, *"Well, I have seen painted buntings, so I know what they look like. I know angels sometimes come in human form to us but I really like how my angels don't have faces."* He seemed to take this as an acceptable answer.

The Outdoor Art Show

It was a bust!

This particular weekend was one of those with distinctive memories. It had many obstacles. I not only had to remember my passion during the weekend, but I also readjusted my thinking based on what I was truly passionate about when it was over. It had been a while since I had participated in an art show, especially an outdoor show. I had forgotten how much work it is. It takes so much time and attention leading up to a show that just lasts a day or two.

What an opportunity it was for me to be invited and accepted into an inaugural art show along the stunning Cibolo Creek in Boerne, Texas. When I make decisions on where and how to sell my art, I spend time praying and asking God for direction. The rain chances for this particular weekend were 40%. I expected a few sprinkles during the day, but not a flood. One of my anchors on this journey is faith. I have faith that with each step the things I cannot see will come to pass. When asking God if this art show was one I should attend, I believe I heard a clear, "Yes!" Branching out to new territory near the bigger city of San Antonio seemed to be a good idea.

Preparing the inventory for this particular show was labor intensive. When I think about it, really all shows are labor intensive. For this one, we prepared our new giclee prints of the sunflowers and My Man designed a new type of frame for these little 8x8 beauties. These same sunflowers had also made their way onto sweet notecards.

Oh, the labor of notecards—folding the clear plastic molded pieces into a box with tabs tucked inward, then folding three unique notecards at the fold line from the packaging and stuffing them carefully into the clear plastic boxes. This is just a behind-the-scenes glimps. Every piece and every product takes this much detail.

Next, we traveled the hour and ten minutes to get to the town and unload both vehicles with art and supplies and a tent and display racks and tables and chairs and easels and paints. It is quite a bit of work for two retirees. Then we set up everything and were ready for the customers. As we set up we had a few sprinkles of rain. I moved several of the larger paintings under the awning to keep them dry. We made two small sales. I don't judge the success of my day based on sales, but the weather was clearly keeping people home. And we do all of this for the people that we might have a chance to meet.

And then the rain came. Not just a few sprinkles, but a deluge of rain. And the wind came along with the rain. Paintings were flying over as our extra tarp was protecting some of our artwork. And did I say our tent did NOT have walls, it was really just an awning? So things got wet. Very wet. The art show was over. We loaded up everything wet into our two vehicles to take home to dry in our garage. The route from our booth location to our cars was up a muddy incline in the rain where we had to reload everything.

After this show, I knew that it was too much to be consistent in attending outdoor art shows. What was I passionate about? Relationships, painting, telling people about the Good News. Art shows were not the most suited way to go about that for Wayman and me. Stick with your passion. Don't do what everyone else is doing. Do what works for you and do what makes you excited. Not every event is a success. But we are not quitting. We will continue to follow our passions. We just are NOT doing many (or any!) more out of town outdoor art festivals.

My Walking Friend

The story of God gifting me with a surprising relationship

This lady is a walker. She walks at least five miles a day. From one end of the town to the other. I met her on the very first day I painted in November 2017 on the sidewalk. She was a breath of fresh air. She was genuine. She cared. I could feel it coming from her spirit. Every day I painted she came by on my side of the street. She told me she leaves her apartment around 7:15 a.m. every morning to start her walk. She goes to the other side of town to the health food store, the large grocery store and other stops along the way. She likes to be home before it gets too hot. She has her plastic bag that she carries her food purchases in back to her apartment. She always stops to visit for a minute. We all want to be seen and this friend stops for the one. The one is me.

> In March when I was painting I heard the whisper, *"Give her a 'Guardian Angel' painting."*
>
> So I asked her, *"If I give you a painting, do you have a place for it?"*
>
> She responded, *"I sure do."*

So I selected the "Guardian Angel", a beautiful 8x8 giclee print.

I asked her if she wanted me to add some additional gold paint to the halo and to the heart of the angel. She said, *"Yes!"* So I added some sparkle and gold shimmer to this angel. She had to hold it out of the bag so it would dry on her walk home.

The next time I saw her she told me she had hung her angel in her living room. She said that when people come over to visit her they can see her "Guardian Angel" hanging on her wall. She is so proud of it. And I am so blessed to have a friend I can count on to stop and visit a minute.

She has a story that I don't know. Yet. But God knows and I am privileged to call her my walking friend.

As time has progressed, our business and our passion has been refined and even redefined. God's passion is our driving force and our voice of encouragement on this journey. When I think about my passion, I think of the surprises God has placed along the way, like my beautiful relationship with my "walking friend." It is worth it. My passion will not die. I will keep pressing onward with action to put as much heart, mind, body and soul into my art and ministry as possible.

Reflections and Action Steps

• Reflect on your top three passions in life. Look for the thread of God's direction interwoven with these passions. Can you see it?

• Ask God for the next steps to expand your passions to the new places He wants to use the gifts He has given you.

Pictured: Sara and her "walking friend"

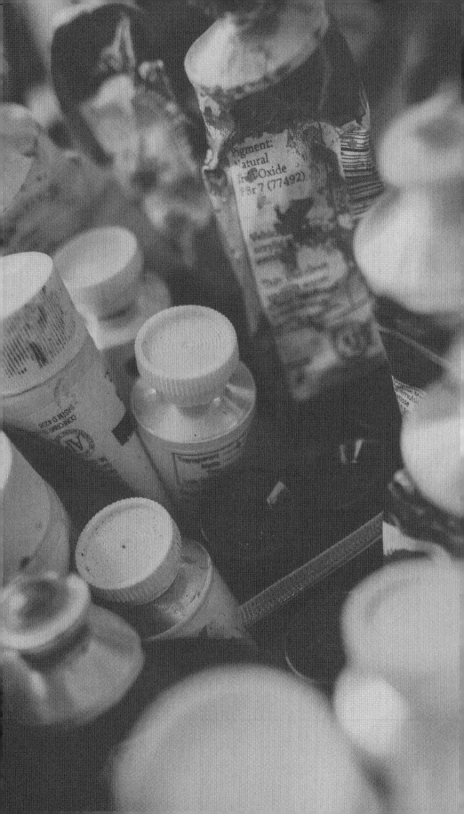

chapter
eight

God knows what is underneath. You are safe.

Balance the Layers

We all have so many pulls in our lives. This way, that way. How can we balance it all? Find where the physical, emotional, and spiritual have a rhythm of life so joy and peace can equally reside. Sounds easier than it is. Some say to push in, others say live simpler. This season of growing into an artist has taken thoughtful contemplation to find my rhythm of rest with Jesus as my Center, my Plumb Line. I have to make daily decisions on my sleep patterns, rest, friends, play time, painting, time with Jesus, time on social media. There are many layers, and just like planting in my garden, if I plant too early or too late, the squash bugs may hatch, or the freeze may come. Whether I am sowing in the ground with seeds or buying established plants, many factors determine the harvest. I have to listen to God. The process is more important than the final product. Each layer has value. Each day and each decision has a ripple effect on the harvest.

Relationships for the Win

It was not about the art

With every step of my journey, God continues to show me that my relationship with Him and with others are critical components. Again, I have to release my expectations of myself and others to embrace the expectancy of the goodness of God. I knew God had arranged for me to be accepted as an artist in the Atlanta art show in late January 2019. Through connections and relationships via Instagram, I was accepted into the show. Because of my own expectations, I thought I would sell out. God had dropped this show into my lap, of course He was going to use it in a mighty way to expand this art business. That was my expectation. I had even brought an extra suitcase full of art to replenish throughout the week-long show.

It was not about the art.

God was taking me deeper. That week I came face to face with my own worth. Was it based on the number of paintings I sold or based on who my Father says I am? See, the battle in my mind. I have to consistently take every thought captive and realign it with the truth of God. The balance of faith (believing with confidence what I can't yet see) and the balance of reality. By the end of the show, two of my smaller pieces sold. I was disappointed and humbled. But God had gone before me. It was not about the art.

In the summer of 1972, I spent four weeks in northern Minnesota at our church summer camp. A surfer girl from the beaches of Florida, Donna Buck (now Wilcox), was my bunkmate. I was the country girl from Texas who could ride a horse and she was the girl who could ride the waves. We became lifelong friends. I was fourteen and she was fifteen.

We went on adventures together, hiking and river rafting in Colorado. We took trips back and forth between Florida and Texas. We even spent our freshman year of college together. I was her maid of honor in her wedding.

And life went on for each of us and our families without any connections.

Then, about eight years ago, we reconnected. Retirement for Donna and her husband, David, brought them to the Blue Ridge Mountains of north Georgia. They have a small organic farm with chickens, goats and a garden.

Since I was coming to Atlanta for the *Spotlight on Art* show in late January 2019, Donna met me at the airport and we spent the week together. One night in Atlanta for the show, then to the mountains and her farm for a few days, and back to Atlanta for the final weekend of the art show. We laughed and talked and enjoyed our deep friendship of over 46 years.

During that week I learned that something was wrong with Donna's left side. We both thought it was a pinched nerve. Within the month Donna was diagnosed with a cancerous brain tumor and has since had surgery to remove the tennis ball size growth in her brain. She is declaring 100% recovery and is back on her little piece of heaven on earth farm. She is fighting with all she has and asking God for a miracle as she goes through intense treatment fighting brain cancer.

It was not about the art show. It is always about God reconnecting our hearts to be in relationship and to give strength and love in times of need. God is always working behind the scenes and going in front of us. Our rear guard is His glory. The ripple effects of His love are never-ending. It is in the first layer, the final layer, and every layer in between.

Using Paints

My painting technique is unique and has been completely discovered through worship and the leadership of Creator God. I describe my style as primitive with abstract aspects. Layering is my hallmark. I use a palette knife and very few brushes. The final touches are made with a wooden skewer stick. There are very few other tools I need to create most of my pieces. I paint in layers and have between five and twelve paintings going at the same time. I love choosing the background colors. That's how I begin each painting. Then, I paint the robes and angel faces on the next layer. My faces don't have features, just shading. The last few layers are the wings, halo and highlights to the heart. Sometimes I also add highlights to the robe. Then, I get one of my favorite painting tools, a wooden skewer stick, and roll it in the paint and then use the edges of the stick to leave the dark brown paint (raw umber) along the outside edges of the angel wings, body and robe. This final touch just makes my heart so happy. I love how it makes the angel reach a new level of beauty.

I love texture. During my first 100 day journal, I began to notice texture in nature. Because of my skill level, I did not know how to use color or shading to create depth. And I love depth and texture. So I created it in a different way than most trained artists. My very first layer is a thick gesso that I comb onto the canvas with a small plastic combing tool. One of the combs has teeth close together and the other has them a bit further apart. Both of these are part of my essential tool kit. After scraping on the thick white gesso, I let the canvas dry at least 24 hours before I put any background layers on. Sometimes I know what my subject will be and I use my

God is always working behind the scenes and going in front of us. Our rear guard is His glory. The ripple effects of His love are never-ending.

palette knife to create an angel's body and wings within the first layer on the canvas. But many times I just scrape on a design and let the subject emerge as I layer in stages.

When I paint on wood I do not add the thick gesso as a first layer since the wood already has so much texture. I paint backgrounds on at least five canvases or wood pieces at a time to get started and then come back to them to add the subjects. On wood, I use distinct palette knife strokes in my first background layers and build on top of that. I use a wonderful thick structured white paint from Australia for my angel wings and for the church and barn highlights. I usually add a touch of thick white as the last layer on any of my florals or cacti to show light shining on the subject.

I probably have at least ten different kinds of paints I use in my studio. I have figured out my favorites over time. Trial and error. Now I know exactly what paints I am going to use for each layer. As mentioned earlier, my very first gesso layer is a thick creamy professional gesso from Ultreck. Remember to get the professional grade. It is the texture of soft butter and I love starting out my canvases with this layer.

Then I use house paint. My friend Ann told me that she thought I could use house paint since they are acrylic. Oh, this was a great discovery.

I don't like mixing paint. Most artists learned this skill long ago. It is just something I don't enjoy and don't particularly want to learn or practice in my painting routine. So, I don't mix paint. It's just one less thing that I have to do. I go to the local paint section of the hardware store and look at the lovely designer brochures for home decor. I pick out about ten to twelve colors that already go together, at least according to some home decorator. Then, I go to the swatch section and pick out my favorite shades for florals, angels, churches, barns, or whatever I am currently painting. I just simply pick colors that I think will look good and that make me happy. It is really that simple; one does not have to do what everyone else is doing. I don't over think it. I buy these colors in the little miniature

sample size, preferably not in regular cans that require a paint opener. I love the plastic jars that allow me to see through to the color.

For the next layer, I use regular acrylic paints in the tubes from the art stores. I use a variety of brands. For the wings, I must have the thick Matisse Structure Acrylic paint from Australia. Then, for my gold halos and gold highlights, I love the Liquitex Structure gold.

I first discovered how to apply the thick gesso layer by chance. After my intuitive workshop in May 2016, I was not afraid to layer on paint. I had some 8x8 canvases lying around my house (no studio yet). My friend Ann came to visit after our return from Mongolia in early November 2016. She asked me what I was going to do with those canvases. They had many layers of paint in shades of blue, but no subjects on them. She suggested that I paint something on top of them since they already had a great background. So, I did what she suggested, and soon after I sold my first layered 8x8 angel. And I just kept using this technique.

When I think back to my very first Cultivate session in October 2014, the facilitator Julie took my very, very thickly painted piece home to dry and it took nearly a week. I was layering the very first time I painted with acrylic.

Be aware of what God is saying as you practice. How does it make you feel? What makes your work unique? We are not just to copy another's work. We get to allow God's DNA within each of us to come out as our own personal trademark.

Honoring My Space

It is really that simple; one does not have to do what everyone else is doing.

My first art studio at home from November 2016 till January 2017 was our kitchen table. I would roll up my artwork and keep it on one end of the table so we could have a tiny amount of space at the other end to eat as a family. Then, after a meal, I would roll my paintings and the tarp covering back out and start painting again. My daughter-in-love, Ana, said, *"We need to move your studio into the guest bedroom."* I was unsure if we should, but my family was in agreement that my paints and art needed its own space.

So the entire family made it happen. We moved the bedroom furniture out and moved in a six-foot table that Wayman had made. We covered it with a plastic cloth and then a heavy canvas tarp. We also placed a canvas tarp over the carpet. Wow! This made a world of difference for me to have dedicated space to paint.

I have a lovely large window that faces south, so the natural light is delightful. And I look out at Wayman's workshop, our backyard chicken coop, our backyard orchard and an array of flowers.

Simply having my own space so that I didn't have to set up and then tear down my work area multiple times a day helped me to further view myself as an artist. I respected my craft and my space enough to dedicate a place to create. It simplified things. It gave me an inspiring place to work and it brought another touch of excellence to my art. It brought more balance.

As I started to honor my space at home, I also began to honor my art. I really believed I needed to cast my net wide. I sold pieces in many different places so that I could learn where my art would sell. Slowly I began to reign it in while still staying flexible. What worked in one location may not work in another.

Some of the places I have sold my art: the local Senior Citizens Craft Shop, local Christmas bazaars, Facebook, Instagram, my online store on my website [28], the monthly outdoor Market Day in our little town of Wimberley, as a guest artist in local galleries, juried art shows in my local Wimberley Valley Art League, art festivals, local co-op art galleries, friends, family, neighbors, open houses, art shows, and word of mouth. And, of course, my best location has been the women's clothing boutique in a Texas Hill Country tourist town, Loca on Main. What a beautiful open door that has been. My art helps to decorate their walls, and painting in front of the store brings in customers for both of us.

Some of those markets are not really ways we sell art anymore. Outdoor out-of-town art shows, no thank you. Etsy, nope. Our local Market Days isn't something I do anymore, either. Things can ebb and flow. Some things will work out, others won't. I can't cling tightly to the things that aren't working because I may miss another opportunity that will present itself later. My recent concentrated efforts are my online art sales from my website, Instagram, FaceBook, Twitter and Pinterest. I will continue to look for any open door, maybe even be a partially open door, and knock on it. The worst thing that I could be told is, *"No."* And if I don't ask, then it is already a *"No!"*

---

[28] actsoneeightblessings.com

Black Friday

A story of authenticity and doubt

Really, what a horrible name for the largest retail day in the United States. The day after our national holiday dedicated to giving thanks. This irony is not lost on my heart. Thanksgiving is my favorite family holiday. I have so many great memories of kickball, Mama's cornbread dressing and giblet gravy. These family gatherings were dedicated to feasting and recalling our greatest blessings of the year.

I also remember the protection God provided when the rabid fox bit my leg some 18 years ago. These are my unique Thanksgiving memories.

November 2018 I worked most of the week leading up to Thanksgiving painting at the storefront in Fredericksburg. I was driven to be there for customers who were getting a jump on Christmas gifts. So ironic. So telling of the condition of my heart. On the Wednesday before Thanksgiving, I was at Loca on Main all day painting. Not a single sale. Not even a set of notecards. Nothing.

God and I have the same dialogue every time my sales for the day, or week or month do not match up to my expectations. As if my joy is dependent on a number. Now, there is nothing wrong with excitement when I have a big sale. God is blessing me. It is way cool. But if my joy is dependent on the big sale, then my heart is entirely in the wrong place.

Pictured: art set-up outside Loco on Main

Sometimes I am afraid that the lack of sales means I'm doing something wrong. What if it means I need to change something, listen harder, DO something? A whirlwind of insecurity. The book of Habakkuk in the Old Testament says even when the barns are empty of cows, the sheep are dying in the fields and there are no olives on the trees, we should still praise God. We should be found rejoicing. [29] This passage of scripture has been a strong marker for me to measure my own praise quotient. This dilemma and my heart's condition were tested big time on Black Friday.

I woke up on Friday morning, right after a beautiful Thanksgiving Day celebration, confused and in need of direction. I was even wondering if I was supposed to go to Fredericksburg to paint. What was my purpose? I mean, after all, family is really really important to me. And I was going to get up and leave them for the day to go to make money? I began to question my priorities. I did not want to go paint. To be among throngs of people on the crowded sidewalk. Just let me read and rest and play with my people and go for a walk and eat some more turkey and dressing.

When in need, ask for help. Before I even started getting ready I asked Wayman to pray for me and help me process my doubts. He prayed for me as we sat on the bed. He asked for sales, for a renewed purpose and for God to send me the people that He wanted me to talk to. And then My Man said to me, "Yes, of course you are going to paint! It is Black Friday! The biggest retail sales day of the entire year!" His prayers gave me strength and helped me to recenter. So I got up and in obedience drove the thirty miles from Harper to Fredericksburg. I went to paint on the biggest retail day of the year.

But the most important work of the day was the transformation of my heart.

And God met me there. I was relaxed and enjoyed meeting my customers. I remembered the year before. Black Friday was the first time I painted in public. I was a mess of nerves and exhausted at the end of that first day.

On this day I worked from about 10 am to 6 pm and sold nearly $500 of art. It was a good day. But the most important work of the day was the transformation of my heart. God sent me specific people, once again, who needed to experience His unfailing love. How easy it is for me to forget my purpose.

---

[29] Habakkuk 3:17 NLT

While I was helping another customer inside the store, I came out to observe someone bent down and going through my paints where I was set up in the threshold of the double doors. I immediately felt compassion and was not bothered. God had sent someone to renew my purposes of art and ministry. This person had been an artist but was unable to paint due to pain and hurt over past "stuff." Telling my testimony of how I recently became an artist, I began to share my techniques and how I go about my processes. Tears flowed. She said to me, *"My mom told me yesterday I had lost my spark. Talking to you and spending time with you has helped me realize I have a little spark coming back."* Prayers were released to the throne room of God. Prayers for healing and blessing and joy and peace and painting to return. I felt the nudge to give her a 5x7 print of my first encaustic angel entitled, *"My Beautiful One."*

She thanked me and explained *"We don't normally park where we parked today, but we had to walk right by this store. I know I was supposed to meet you today."* What a privilege to be partnering with God to release hope and love into this new friend. God is so amazing to layer hope and clarity at multiple levels, for my heart and for my new friend's heart. I went home thanking God for lifting my head and giving me renewed vision. He opened my ears and my eyes for His purposes right when I needed it. God gave me several more opportunities on Friday to love on customers who had fractured life stories. God's strength became my strength.

So, with my eyes on Jesus, I can find the balance. Finding that rhythm of rest doesn't mean I don't struggle with the balance some days. But when I keep my eyes on Jesus and listen to His quiet whispers (and to My Man), I can take the next step in faith.

"Thy Kingdom Come, Thy Will Be Done"

A story of rebuilding and reconciliation within my family

In May 2018, my family of origin had a reunion with 40 plus immediate family members. I knew I needed to bring angel paintings as gifts to each of my sisters-in-law as a symbol of refreshed love. I had heard God tell me to bring enough paintings for each sister-in-law to choose one. Even for my ex-sisters-in-law. Since this was our first family reunion in more than ten years, it was a time of healing, refreshing and new beginnings. It was a time to celebrate the memories of our parents. The gathering was planned beautifully by my nephews.

Even the cooking happened without a gunfight or cussing match, which is a miracle all its own.

If any family needed to have a reunion of hurt hearts, it was ours. As with most families, we have some messy, broken stuff. Specifically, Forgiveness. My family of origin has taken big steps toward embracing God's beautiful plan of forgiveness. There has been such freedom in this healing process. And it could not have been complete without barbecued goat meat, beef brisket and Mama's famous chocolate sheet cake.

During the reunion, I made sure that each sister-in-law was able to pick an angel to take home with her. One sister-in-law, Elizabeth, recently wrote in her own words what her chosen angel named, "Thy Kingdom Come, Thy Will Be Done" means to her:

> "Sara, The day you gave me the angel we were at a family reunion. I was on chemotherapy for pancreatic cancer and had a broken right arm with a shattered bone just below the shoulder. I didn't know it was shattered at the time, although I had a feeling it was. I just knew it hurt and was doing my best to ignore it. I wasn't very excited about getting a painting but took one anyway. I chose one with a lot of turquoise and bright color. At home I hung it just inside the front door, and, truth be told, mostly forgot about it. Later, I was talking to our sister-in-law, Carolyn, and she mentioned how much she liked hers and that when she looked at it she always felt very positive. Talking with her made me look at mine again, and I realized mine gave me very positive feelings, also. I just wanted you to know that it has helped me with the things I've had to cope with this year. Sometimes when I look at it I see you and know that you are supporting me with prayer and encouragement. It is a very positive thing in my life. Thank you."

Elizabeth has completed her chemo treatment for pancreatic cancer and has quality of life way past her diagnosis. She is a living miracle. About 75% of people diagnosed with pancreatic cancer die within the first year of diagnosis. Praise be to God for His love that never ends.

These angel painting gifts helped symbolize of the love of God and our love towards each other. Most of my family did not even know I was an artist. I have to trust God to show me how to release the paintings He helps me to paint, and then sends them to the places He wants them to go. Our family reunion in May 2018 proved to be a happy and healing time for our family.

Sunglasses and An Angel

A story of unexpected love given and received

One Saturday during the summer of 2018 I was painting in Fredericksburg, and a young couple in their late twenties wearing sunglasses stopped where I was painting. The woman told me she loved my paintings and was very drawn to them. I could tell as she looked intently at my artwork and even reached out to touch some of my paintings. I started to tell her the prices of the paintings like I do when I can tell a potential buyer is interested. She quickly told me she did not have money for artwork. I said, *"Cool, no problem."* But they did not walk off after she told me she was not buying any art.

I then heard the whisper from God. *"Give her a painting. Let her choose. I see her. I know her. I love her."* So I quickly went inside the store and chose two paintings for her to choose from. She knew exactly which angel she wanted. I do not remember the name of the one she chose but I could tell it was a holy connection for her. She held it up to her heart. I begin to tell her what I heard God whisper to me about her. *"God sees you. God loves you so much. God is with you. He is your hope. God has not forgotten you."* With sunglasses still on, I could see tears rolling down the cheeks of the young man. I saw tears rolling down the cheeks of the young woman. Then the young man told me that I had no idea how much this painting meant to the woman. He was so grateful. I gave her a hug and said a prayer of blessing over them. They went on their way with a fresh message of love from the Great Creator— a tangible symbol of His love in the form of a 5x7 acrylic angel painting on canvas. I do not take these moments for granted. I know the holy ground I stand on. It is all His art, not my art. This is the true secret to balancing the layers.

I have had to establish healthy rhythms of balance in the process of becoming an artist. Should this be a business or a ministry? Which is more important? What does God want for me? God has shown me the beautiful balance of ministry and business side by side, not competing with each other, but intertwined. In each season I have to trust that God will guide the balance of my art ministry in His perfect rhythm.

Reflections and Action Steps

• How is it going with all the parts of your life—business, spiritual, emotional, physical? Is one draining your cup more than others?

• Think about the next three months of your life. Does anything need to be adjusted to get in better alignment to balance in your life?

chapter
nine

We are the story for all eternity.

Document the Journey

The Israelites in the Old Testament went through quite a bit. They had to trust what they could not see. They had to believe that God would do what He said He would do. They went up against armies and situations where it seemed there was no possible way they would make it through alive. I would say the theme that God repeated most through these stories was *"Trust Me"*. And I would say the theme God repeated second most was *"Remember"*.

At one point, God told His people to write down His commandments and tie them to their foreheads, their robes and their doorways. [30] He knew that sometimes we forget. I have the temptation when I am in uncharted territory to be fearful. I can embrace negative thoughts because things aren't going the way I thought they would. I forget what God has already done for me. I forget that He is trustworthy. I forget that I don't need to be the one in charge.

How can we be sure to remember what God has done? Document the journey. When we document our story we not only have an easier time remembering how God worked in our life, but we can also share our story easier with others. God loves stories. The Old Testament is full of stories about God's people. Jesus throughout the Gospels uses stories to teach lessons. Our stories encourage others and bring glory to the One who gave us our story. We need to remember what He has done and we need to tell others.

All of these techniques I have shared, the way we run our business, the testimonies of how this art has spoken to others, do not need to be hidden. I don't want to hoard this knowledge so that no one else can

---

[30] Deuteronomy 6:8-9 NIV

God loves stories. reproduce it. I want to share it. It is for you as much as it is for me. Two years before the release date of this book God whispered that I needed to write down my story. A year before the release date He said it again. I obeyed Him, and now people are encouraged by the working of the Holy Spirit through the story of this little art business from the Texas Hill Country.

This journey in particular has been documented in two ways, through words and through art. I can see how God has moved this story of His from the very first art pieces I made in Cultivate to the pieces that are now all over the world from Texas to Russia.

The Day After Black Friday

A story of how I received hope when I needed it

Wayman's prayers were heard and answered so strongly on Friday after Thanksgiving 2018. So, I asked him again to pray for me and release God's love through me on Saturday before I left for Loca on Main to paint. He prayed again for our God in heaven to move mightily through this art and bring the people He wanted to reach. I also requested that he pray for sales, and I specifically asked for an encaustic painting to sell on Saturday. I love the encaustic pieces. I just can't justify making these pieces if they are not selling because creating this type of art takes more time and resources than acrylic painting.

Before lunch I had a married couple drawn to my artwork and they listened to the story of how I became an artist. They perused my art both in the store and on the sidewalk. They eventually decided on two different smaller pieces of art for their two children. It was such a sweet time with them. Once they made their selections, I showed them to the counter to pay and went back outside to paint.

A few minutes later, I looked up and they were carrying another painting, a 20x20 titled _"I Will Leave This House Singing."_ They had bought three pieces of art. God blew my mind with His goodness.

And then the real purpose behind our meeting became clear. On their way out this couple asked me, _"How do you do it? What are your happy marriage secrets?"_ They confided in me that they were having trouble in their marriage. Tears filled their eyes.

I looked at this painting. It was from May 2017. When I painted it God already knew who would buy it. I shared my secrets of our blessed marriage for over 33 years—of serving each other, forgiving quickly, maybe even forgetting, and then learning to trust again. All with God in the center. They declared, *"This painting will hang in our living room. We believe this painting was meant for us!"*

I asked them if I could pray for them. They quickly agreed, and I laid my hands on their shoulders and asked God to rebuild and refresh their commitment to each other. He is the Restorer. Again, I experienced a deep renewed purpose of my art.

And to top off the day, a new customer bought one of my encaustic angels. Oh God, thank You for making the way. Thank You for hearing my prayers and My Man's prayers. Clarity came like a flood.

Pictured: "I Will Leave This House Singing"

God sent me the people He wanted to be touched. And in return, I was reminded so powerfully of my assignment and purpose to share hope and encouragement through my art.

Spoken Words

When I started this process I was totally unaware of the power of words over my life. The very first prophetic word spoken over my art that I can remember was my dear friend, Judy Bennet, who was a part of that first Cultivate group. One day as we were in the circle to talk about our processes, Judy declared to me that I would have my paintings in a gallery someday and have my own art shows. I laughed at her and said, *"No way!"* I have since learned not to have negative responses to those types of positive statements. Instead, I bring them to God, write them down, repeat them and believe that they are part of my destiny and legacy.

At our current church, we had an activation class on releasing the prophetic in our lives and to others. One of my new friends from this class, Marqita Wolber, told me that she had a vision of me writing names on the back of my paintings. She said these names were prophetic statements that would speak to those who received the paintings. I took this as confirmation that I was exactly where I needed to be since she did not know that I do that already. Many times I hear the names of the paintings through the current worship music I am listening to or the scriptures I have just read. I am just now beginning to understand the power of the titles I give each painting. I actually participated in this prophetic transfer for more than a year before I realized I was even doing it. I know now God releases His love through the paintings and the names they carry.

In this same prophetic activation class, another new friend, Dana Sleger, had a prophetic word for me. She saw me standing in the center of a room with many pieces of art all around me. I took my brush and painted on each painting as I danced and walked around the room. In her vision, she also saw that each painting had a name and that these names carried power with them to each new owner. Dana knew that I was an artist, but she didn't have any details about my style, technique, or process. She had no idea that I painted many paintings at the same time, or that I named each one. But God knew and told her about me in a vision. The love of God was so evident while hearing the visions that He was giving to those around me. It was as if He were whispering to me *"I see you. I love you. I am working through you. Keep doing what you are doing."*

"New Mercies Every Morning"

A story of how an angel painting became a turning point in the grief process

Mary and Bill stood speechless in front of my angel paintings on the sidewalk. Tears were flowing and words were not. I waited.

Mary said to me, *"I want every one of these angels."*

And then I waited again. They told me they were driving by in their car, saw my angel paintings from the street and had to turn around to come back to the angels. Something was pulling them to the art. I knew it was Jesus. He was waiting and ready to bring them the comfort they had been waiting for. Their sweet Brittany had passed from this life over two years ago. Their grief was still deep and wide. They took their time looking for an angel. They told me their Brittany had light brown hair. She was their extra special daughter with the extra chromosome. She had lived until age 30.

I said, *"Let's go inside the store and look. I think there is one that is perfect in here."*

Bill walked over to a shelf, and there she was. He said, *"This is the angel."* Mary agreed quickly. A sweet round face, light brown hair, soothing shades of blues and grays. *"New Mercies Every Morning"* had found her new home. They knew the minute they saw this angel that she would remind them of their Brittany.

This is a story I could not write myself. God wrote this love story. I had painted *"New Mercies Every Morning"* in April 2017. With all my heart and soul, I believe that God knew that Bill and Mary would find this angel in August 2018 as a symbol of His comfort over the loss of their beautiful daughter. I asked them if I could pray for them. They readily agreed. We stood on the sidewalk praying and crying. I thanked God for Brittany's parents, and I thanked Him for choosing them to be her parents. We hugged and cried and knew that God was there with us.

It seemed as if this angel painting was going to be a turning point. Two years of deep grief could now change over to a new level of comfort and peace. I am sure we will never know what was happening in the spiritual realm. But Jesus Himself said, "Blessed are those who mourn, for they shall be comforted." [31] All three of us were blessed by the working of the Holy Spirit in this moment.

---

[31] Matthew 5:4 ESV

"O, Holy Ones"

A story of surprises and hope found in one painting

I never know who will walk by on Main Street. I never know who will stop. Many keep walking. A few stop to watch. A few stop to ask questions. I am learning to listen and to not overwhelm the potential customer with my words. I am a talker. God continues to teach me greater discernment in sharing my story. In the beginning, my habit of talking and talking about my own art journey took priority over listening. Now I talk less and ask to hear other's stories. This interaction builds connections and relationships.

I know God sets up holy intersections time after time with my art and my story of the impossible. I trust Him. I pray to be used to bring hope and love and joy and encouragement to those He sends on the sidewalk. Just like the Israelites, I forget so easily His miracles and the

Pictured: "New Mercies Every Morning"

> *I know God sets up holy intersections time after time with my art and my story of the impossible.*

impossible happening before my eyes. But when I forget He sets up another holy intersection.

This particular mom found a parking space right in front of the boutique where I was painting. I remember seeing her get out with her son. They walked down the street to shop at the Christmas store. I could tell that he had special needs. After about thirty minutes or so they came back. Her son got into the car, into his safe place. I can still hear clearly the mom ask me with fingers pointing to the painting on the easel,

"Is that painting for sale?"

I replied, "Yes, it is. I am not finished it with yet unless you want me to be finished. It has no wings and no gold."

She replied, "I love it just the way it is. Can you leave it like this?"

"Of course, but can I sign it and name it?" I asked. God, tell me the name You have for this painting. I heard, "O, Holy Ones."

When I told her the price, it was more than her budget. I heard the whisper of God to give her a discounted price and knock $75 off. I asked her if she could afford the lower price and she could. I knew this painting was for her.

"O, Holy Ones" was full of more abstract figures than normal. It was one of the characteristics of the painting she loved because there was no empty space.

Twenty four figures on this 12x36, a size of canvas known to intimidate me in previous days of painting. I didn't even know how to use space on a canvas this size. I had used this size only once about six months prior. But on this particular morning, I pulled out this gessoed canvas and said to myself, "Today is the day to paint on this canvas."

God had lead me to deal with my fears and to take risks. So I used this canvas, which had a wire on the back and was ready to be hung thanks

to My Man. This canvas had been in the back room of the boutique for at least eight weeks, passed over until this day. I had started with shades of gray and dark brown, with abstract faces, hair and bodies. These abstract figures were painted from the top edges of the painting to the bottom corners.

No wings, no gold, but complete. It was new for me to stop before I was finished, but the foundational layers were enough. Listening to Father was more important than what I thought should have been the finished product.

After I helped her carry the painting to her car, I asked her if I could pray for her. She expressed she could feel hope and joy coming off of me from Jesus and Holy Spirit. Just arriving in Fredericksburg after a five-hour drive from a city in North Texas with her son, this was her first place to stop and park. A good parking spot is coveted in this little tourist town, and she found one right in front of where I was painting.

Right there on the sidewalk, He infused hope in her heart. And in my heart. He sees us.

She shared pieces of her broken story. Abusive relationships. Impending divorce. Lack of substantial provision. A special needs child requiring constant care. Questions of where to move or where to stay. But God saw her. Right there on the sidewalk, He infused hope in her heart. And in my heart. He sees us. He weaves a story of love between those who were strangers just fifteen minutes earlier.

Pictured: "O, Holy Ones" with its new owner

The next morning, as I was starting to paint on Main Street, she drove by, honked and rolled down her window to say hi! So many layers in this story of God's purposes. Lord, help me not forget these testimonies. I am writing these down so we won't forget His messages of love.

The Perfect Gift in the Most Difficult of Circumstances

A story of comfort being carried in a gift

Many people see my artwork as they drive by from the busy intersection where the boutique is located. Potential customers can see me painting at my easel. I display my paintings outside along the sidewalk and in front of the large windows of the boutique.

One day I looked up from my painting to see a woman with her head bowed looking at my paintings. She said nothing. She was silent. After a few minutes, I asked her if I could help her with anything. She had tears in her eyes and told me her best friend's mother had been tragically killed in a car accident the previous night. She and her best friend both had daughters who were also best friends, and she didn't know how she was going to tell her own daughter the details from the night before. She drove by and saw my angel paintings. She knew she had to stop and buy an angel gift for her friend to bring comfort in the midst of such deep grief. After she bought the angel she told me she was so thankful she had seen my artwork. In fact, she just parked right in front of the store in a space that was not an official parking place.

As she was leaving the store, I asked her if I could pray for her. She agreed. We stood right outside the doors on the sidewalk and prayed to a God who sees everything, who sends friends to help us in times of need. I asked God to use her as a sign of comfort even when words were not needed, and I asked that she would carry peace into the situation as she loved on her friend. I also asked that her daughter be able to love on her little friend whose grandmother had died. The angel painting would not take the sting of death away. But the angel would symbolize comfort and love as a tangible sign of comfort in the most tragic of circumstances.

Each painting itself is a testament to the goodness of God. Each painting has its own story and is woven into the fabric of its forever home. And, of course, each painting is also woven into my story. Each brush stroke, each name, each prayer further documents the journey.

Reflections and Action Steps

• We cannot be the overflow and tell our story unless we are healed and filled up by God. What step do you need to take to document your own story? Who are you sharing your story with?

• Think about others God has put in your path that need to hear your story. Think big! Take a step forward to make it happen. Is it a book? A blog? A piece of art? A cup of coffee with a new friend?

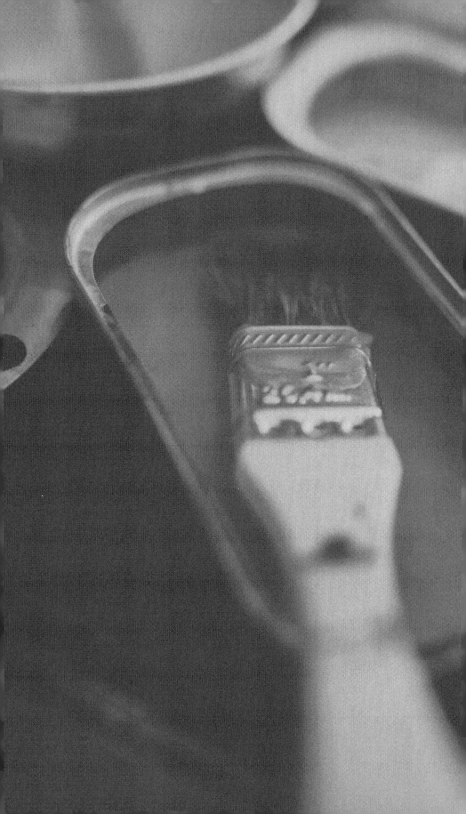

chapter
ten

We are never finished, always in process.

Hold it all Lightly

Each new year I pray for a scripture. God gives me a specific verse to have and hold throughout the year that reflects what God is doing in my life. My verse for 2018 was profound and applicable. *"Never doubt God's mighty power to work in you and accomplish all this. He will achieve infinitely more than your greatest request, your most unbelievable dream, and exceed your wildest imagination! He will outdo them all, for His miraculous power constantly energizes you."* [32] More than you can dream or imagine, not according to man's view but God's economy. How poignant is this? It was just what my heart needed to hear over and over again as I trusted Him and took step after step into this journey of becoming an artist.

After He told me this verse, I continued to hear Him speak. I wrote it down in what I call a *"Jesus Stream."* It is as if I were in a one-way dialogue and Holy Spirit deposits information for me to hear. That day He continued: *"For all that I have is yours. I keep my promises. This is for My Kingdom. You are a light bringer. I will send you to dark places but My light in you will overcome the darkness. I have this plan. It is My plan. Not yours. You are creating to bring heaven to the ends of the earth. Just like with this book, you heard Me. 'Write right now.' And you did. And you are. I have all the details. Trust me."*

What does the future of Acts 1:8 Blessings hold? I don't know. But I know God is good. He keeps His promises. I can trust Him. This all belongs to Him. I am blessed beyond words to have learned to worship Him with color and shape and texture. This art world is a world of wonder. This is adventure, my friends.

---

[32] Ephesians 3:20 TPT

"You Are My Delight"

My story of the week leading up to paint for the first time at Bethel Austin

"How do I get your painting of the sunflowers? I have to have it!" Tears streamed down her reddened face. She was holding a tissue. This young woman came up to me when I stepped off the stage after my first time painting prophetic art during worship at my new church, Bethel Austin. Another small beginning. I've been collecting them. When I think too small, He is thinking big. When I start to think too big, He brings me back to another small beginning. It is a balance, and it is not my job to control it. It is my job to hold it lightly. When I hold it lightly, my own expectations give way to what He really wants to do. And what He has planned is always better than what I have planned.

Three days before I met this young woman, and three days before I painted for the first time as part of the prophetic art worship team I waited in anticipation for God to move. I spent time in prayer in preparation for painting at church. I even asked a friend, Julie, earlier in the week to pray for God's love to connect to what I painted in unexpected ways. About ten years prior, Julie had experienced a holy encounter with a piece of art painted during worship while visiting Bethel Redding Church. She saw a piece of art during worship and then shortly afterward, on the flight home, she saw the exact little girl who had been portrayed in the painting. This is the kind of holy intersection God brings. My prayer was that He would use my art in ways that would bring holy encounters to others, so I invited Julie to come alongside and pray with me. Do it again, God. Speak to someone in the congregation. Oh, yes. My first small step of obedience. I had to learn to trust that I would hear Him loud and clear for the entire process. I felt like I was stepping out to risk hearing God in new ways.

Two days prior to painting on stage at our church during worship, six college students all needed words of encouragement. During the two-hour drive it took to get there, I heard God tell me that while I was with these students I needed to practice my gift of prophecy. My task was to share with them how much they are loved and to give them a specific word or encouragement. I asked the college students while sitting around the living room,

> *"Hey, can I take chance with giving y'all a word of prophecy?*
> *I feel like God wants me to share encouragement with each*

one of you. I have never done it with a room full of people. I am new at this."

They all responded, *"Yes. We want to hear!"* It was holy and God gave me words, specific words, for each one as I moved from one student to the next. I started talking and then God poured out of my mouth the liquid gold.

Some of the different words I shared:

> *You are a leader. Every job from your past work experience is in preparation for the leadership positions you will hold in the future. You are excellent in your work as a servant.*

> *God loves the gifts He has given you, and expect more to start surfacing. These gifts will enable you to become an expert in new areas. Be aware of these new areas of interest because God is going to start growing them.*

> *You are so gentle but yet so strong with purpose for the Kingdom.*

> *I see you as a precious baby, taking your first steps. Papa God is clapping for you. He sees you and is so excited about your progress. Papa hears you say your first words. He sees you walk across the stage at your high school graduation. He is cheering you on. And He sees you get your college diploma. He loves you so much and He is your Papa. He is so proud of you.*

Later that evening I discovered that the student I shared that last word with lived in thirteen different foster homes and never had a solid father figure. God loves His children, plain and simple. What a blessing to step out in faith, learn to practice this new gifting and to encourage a young Believer all at the same time. The words still ring in my ears, *"Yes, I was present in every stage and I am with you always."*

Then one girl timidly raised her hand and said,

> *"I have a word for you, too. Can I share what I heard?"*

> *"Yes! Please share!"* I responded.

> *"I heard God telling me...Sara, you know how to love well. You have been doing it your whole life. But I wanted you to*

reach other people. To love other people that could not be reached in normal ways. I have given you the ability to be an artist to reach people that would not be reached in other ways. I have given you the ability to paint so you can share My love with more people."

I took a deep breath and received this word. It was a surprise. And just before my eyes, God released more of His love through this precious college student. That was her small beginning.

Twenty four hours before this specific worship time I knew I needed to prepare my canvases. Two canvases needed the first layer of gesso so they could start drying. I applied the thick creamy gesso with a comb onto the 20x24 canvases, one in the form of an angel and one with a pattern for three flowers. *"Am I to have two prepared? Are these the subjects You want me to paint?"*— it seemed as if this was a constant dialogue between Creator God and me.

Twelve hours before I hear the word *"delight"* come into my thoughts. *"God, is this my word for the day?"*

I had been asking Him for a fresh word every day for a few months prior. This practice anchors me to His voice and purpose. It gracefully floated like a butterfly into my thoughts even before I read scripture or began to pray. *"Delight."* Yes, this was my word for the day. *"What about 'delight'?"* I asked Him in confirmation.

"I DELIGHT" in you. Receive My delight today. Yes, you are My delight!" Was His response. So I agreed with this word in my spirit and just had a sense of calmness come over me. He delights in these little moments. *"Paint the angel and flowers and delight in the process. Enjoy. I have made this day for you."* Finally, the confirmation I had been waiting for.

Three hours till I paint. As I drove to Austin I asked Father for scripture for these two pieces. I searched for scriptures related to *"delight"* on my favorite Bible app. This app has a great word search feature and allows users to easily compare different translations. I was lead to Psalm 91:14 *"...because you have delighted in Me..."* for the angel and Song of Songs 2:3 [33] *"...I blossom in His shade, ...resting with delight where His glory never fades..."* for the floral.

The time had come, my first time to paint on stage during worship while letting God lead me to prophetically paint what He desired. It is clear

---

[33] TPT

looking back that God had led me to paint each and every painting, but this was different. The others were prophetic on *"accident"* and these two were prophetic on purpose. What if I don't hear God correctly, what if I have the scripture wrong? He hadn't left me yet, He wasn't going to leave me now.

First, I prayed and surrendered the time into God's hands while standing and kneeling on stage. Then, I wrote the verse with charcoal on the angel canvas and began to paint the first layers of the angel. I set the angel aside to let the first layers dry. Then I placed the floral on the easel to write Song of Songs 2:3 on the back.

Leah told me that her eyes welled up with tears when she saw me write her life verse on the canvas. Worshippers were up front singing, dancing and lifting up the name of Jesus in praise while I was painting on stage.

I asked Him and heard each step to take. He told me to start with brown paint on the floral. Leah loves sunflowers. Her favorite flower. When she saw the brown circles go on, she asked God for it to be a sunflower painting. And when she watched me add the orange and yellow petals, she lost it. Jesus encountered His beautiful daughter with such a strong and powerful message of love through this sunflower painting named, *"You Are My Delight!"*

He takes His love and delight in us and spreads it thick, like the first layer of gesso on the canvas.

While I was looking for confirmation for my painting, Leah was looking for confirmation for what was next for her. She wanted to move in obedience. This was God's response to her prayers. *"God, I want to honor you. What do you want me to do next?"*

His response? *"My darling, you are my delight."* And she also heard Him say that she will be involved in ministry either in Dallas or Florida. He hasn't left her yet, He isn't going to leave her now.

Pictured: Sara with Leah and "You Are My Delight"

119

Leah worked at Chick-Fil-A and told me she could get the money to me by the end of the following month. But I heard God tell me to sow it back into her ministry. This painting was hers. Not only was I to give it to her, but it would be symbolic of providing for her financial needs for her future ministry. This is our God. He takes His love and delight in us and spreads it thick, like the first layer of gesso on the canvas.

"All That I Have Is Yours"

A story of sharing what I have been given

> *"You are different! I can't believe that you are sharing all your secrets as an artist. Most artists never want to share their technique,"* John said to me.

He is an artist in Texas. He and his wife stopped by to chat with me as I painted on the sidewalk in front of Loca on Main. He was in awe of the open hand that I have been taught to have. I have always known this gift is not mine.

There is a story in the Bible of a father that tells his jealous and disappointed son, *"Everything I have is yours."* [34] The impact of this parable on my perspective as an artist has been powerful. The older son was jealous of the younger son, who was being honored at a big party. The younger son had just returned home after living a life in darkness. The father gave the younger son a beautiful robe, new sandals, the family ring and even had the prized fatted calf roasted for them to eat in celebration. [35]

The older son thought he was being ripped off. He thought the younger son was receiving what he had earned. The truth in this story is that the father has it all. He has enough to give away to all of us. He owns the storehouses. The storehouse will never run empty. It was the father's design to make us as designers and creators. It is a gift from the original Designer. The first Creator.

In man's economy, what many would call the *"normal"* way of thinking, these skills need to be protected and hidden because there is not enough. It is a scarcity mentality. Here I was, just a few years ago, with no skill and no idea that creating art would ever be in my future. With each step of the journey He has unveiled the next steps. He always has. He always will show me the next steps.

---

[34] Luke 15:31 NLT, [35] Luke 15:11-32

These gifts of wisdom and revelation came from Him, and that is why I can give them away. It is not a one-time outpouring, but a constant flow of creativity that only continues into eternity. He tells me, *"Everything I have is yours."* He doesn't run out of ideas or ways to create. And since He is the source of all my art, neither will I. I can share Him. All of HIM. God is so generous.

He doesn't run out of ideas or ways to create.

I have crossed paths with many artists who have believed the lies. So many lies. Some for a very long time. Art is a connection between the human soul with the Father's heart. For me, the discovery of God's heart and passion comes through as I paint for Him. It is all connected. I already have filled a book with the stories and testimonies of what God has done. And this story is not ending. It will have many chapters past the publication date. Every day God is writing more of His story in my life. We don't have to cling to it. For the goodness and the promises of God to take full effect on our lives, we need to hold it lightly. Let it be what it is going to be, and learn to follow the Shepherd's voice.

Anna came up to me with a longing look. She wanted to know more. She saw me painting with the Prophetic Art Team that evening at church. I asked her, *"Are you an artist?"*

"No, not really," she replied. We talked. I shared my story. I also suggested that she set aside special time, a sabbath for creating. I suggested maybe fifteen minutes, an ongoing project or to paint different art pieces every day. I told her that it pleases the Father's heart for us to want to be with Him every day.

After sharing and praying with Anna, I asked her, *"Are you an artist?"*

She confidently responded with excitement in her voice, *"Yes, I am!"* Thank You, Jesus, for helping us be all we can for You— carriers of light and love for the kingdom.

The Transition from Small Beginnings to Professional Artist

When do I stop saying I am a new artist? I don't know. I think it is soon. I have been selling for two years now. I have been painting for four years. I have painted over 1000 paintings. I have sold over 900 paintings. I think it is time. I was juried into a large art show in Atlanta, *Spotlight on Art*, the last week of January 2019. This book was to go to print after the show. During the show, I wondered *"Will I have a final story to place in the book as an epilogue after I return from Atlanta?"* While I was in Georgia it became clear that this book needed more time.

A dear friend, Charlotte, told me at my two-year marker of selling my art that I have been found. I am known as an artist. I do not have to wait to be found. I am not even sure what that means when I say it. But what was deemed impossible is now a reality. I am a professional artist. Tears flow as I write this. Me. A country girl who never took an art class. He whispered to my heart four years ago. He also responded when I asked in a whisper my impossible prayer. And here we are. I am not sure when the transition happened. But I do feel like this small beginning is coming to an end and more "small beginnings" are beginning to take flight.

I have completed less than ten encaustic paintings. But I so want many more to come forth with the layers of beeswax and heat between each layer with treasured objects. This book is published. I am now teaching

classes about releasing creativity. I have more books stirring up. Devotional books, children's books. And guess who will be the illustrator for my children's books? God has given me the ability to illustrate my own books. I have dreamt of writing children's books for many years. It will happen.

Pictured: A few of Sara's encaustic paintings

The second part of my impossible prayer on that day in Mongolia in September 2016 was to sell my art and have an art business with net profits of $4000 per month to help people all over the world. I still believe I will see the fulfillment of this prayer. Our gross sales some months are at $4000. In my specific prayer, I asked for the net to be $4000. I know He can do it. He loves Acts 1:8 Blessings. It is all for His glory. Every painting. Every customer. Every interaction. Every Instagram Post. Every gift. Every stroke. Every student. Every reader. It is all His. What a privilege this journey has been. Not in my wildest dreams or imagination could I have concocted this plan. He is literally using my creativity to bring heaven to earth.

It is my passion. It is my purpose. From Uganda to Egypt to Madagascar to Indonesia to China to Mongolia to Russia to Jordan to India to Greece to Macedonia to the British Virgin Islands to Northern Ireland to Kentucky to California to Indiana to Austin to Wimberley and any place in between, we give out God's love. I celebrate the small beginnings. I trust and know my Shepherd's voice. Will you take the next step in your small beginnings? I can think of nothing more beautiful than for this book to help you begin.

Pictured: Sara & Wayman with their entire family

Reflections and Action Steps

• What's next in your journey? What is the next small step to your impossible? Can you take the next step?

• Write down an impossible prayer that God has put on your heart. A prayer that when it is answered only God could have answered it.

Afterword: What's Next

I felt the stirring in my soul to start teaching again a few months ago. I have prayed for five years about the vacant lot next to our home. I wanted to purchase it and build a retreat cottage that offered healing art classes and a studio space. But God had a different plan that slowly unfolded. I have the opportunity to teach classes at a beautiful bed and breakfast in our community, BellaVida Bed & Breakfast and Retreat Center.

When my husband and I went to meet with Belinda, the property owner, in December 2018, I never expected to leave her Bed & Breakfast with three events booked for Spring 2019. But God knew. I booked two classes called *"Practicing Hearing God's Voice in the Creative Process"* for January and February. I also booked a full weekend retreat in early May 2019.

We are also praying for more to happen overseas in other countries. I am specifically asking God to open doors in Northern Ireland, Central Asia, Russia, Australia, and any other place He wants for me to go teach and share my journey.

God has shown me a new stream, which is mentoring one-on-one with others in a virtual setting. This began in early 2019. I have an extensive background in mentoring practices in public school settings. I am using this skill set to assist others on their creative journey. I have named these mentoring sessions *"Developing Your Creative Calling."*

Also on the horizon are e-courses that help people hear God on their journey, children's books, a devotional and open studio time to welcome others to paint in His Presence and even more.

I am still dreaming with God. He is so faithful. He says to us, *"Never doubt God's mighty power to work in you and accomplish all this. He will achieve infinitely more than your greatest request, your most unbelievable dream, and exceed your wildest imagination! He will outdo them all, for His miraculous power constantly energizes you."* [36] May you each embrace the miraculous power of Jesus to accomplish more than you ever dreamed possible in your own life. God is waiting for our next steps because it is the small beginnings toward our impossible dreams.

---

[36] Ephesians 3:20 TPT

About the Author

Sara is known for the joy she carries in whatever she is doing, which happens to include gardening in her backyard with her chickens, taking daily walks with her two dogs, Coda and Chico, and experiencing adventures to the ends of the earth. Now in her early 60's, she is growing as an artist, author, and teacher of hearing God's voice. Recently has been told that she has flunked retirement. Sara worked in Texas public schools in the roles of teacher and principal in the elementary, middle school and central administrative levels. She received her Doctorate in Education in K-12 School Leadership and retired after a successful 24-year career. She now lives in Wimberley, Texas, with her husband, Wayman (My Man). She has two sons, Samuel and Justin, stepson Jared, three daughters-in-love, Rachel, Ana, and Donna, a precious granddaughter, Heba, and an amazing grandson, Jonah.

She welcomes connections and communication on her website, sarathurman.com or actsoneeightblessings.com, where you can also purchase copies of her book, artwork, mentoring packages, retreats, classes and online courses.

Acknowledgments

I had never dreamt of being an author. But I knew this book had to be written. God told me to write and He would take care of the details. And He is great with details.

To my children making the love of Jesus known—

- Samuel, Rachel and sweet baby granddaughter Heba, who are now on the field to love the "one in front of you" on the opposite side of the earth. I am so very proud of you.

- Justin and Ana, who give their lives away every day to those who had lost hope. You love them in powerful ways to show them the arms of hope in Jesus. I am so very proud of you.

- Jared, Donna and Jonah, who breathed life and accolades along the way. It would have been much harder without your cheers.

- "M" and "E", your example of living with purpose every day, far away from Texas, has blessed my own journey of faith.

To my friends in Mongolia and Russia: you have demonstrated to me what living with Jesus truly as your center looks like. You all help make my life radiate with purpose.

The rest belongs to Annie Ward, my brilliant, spirit-filled editor. God loves to bring us surprises, and I never imagined that a conversation in the parking lot of the yoga studio after class would spark the beginning of our mutual relationship with Small Beginnings. Annie, you have been the gift every writer needs to transform what was just mediocre into something excellent. You have the ability to read my thoughts, even though my words were not always clear. You helped to perfectly craft this book from many little stories into a flow of words that captures my full story. I am forever grateful for your willingness to keep working even when I wanted to stop. You are a faithful friend and an editor extraordinaire. This book is your small beginnings as an editor. I pray for many more writers to find your God-given skill set. [37]

To my worshipping, praying, painting, writing Circle of Blessings friends: Julie, Holly, Judy, Tracy, Peggy, Christine, Genevieve, God used you to speak words of life over this infant artist. You saw my tears, you held my heart gently and you believed when I didn't.

To my designer friend: Ashley Davis. You made the outside beautiful and the inside even more beautiful. Your words of encouragement and affirmation in the writing process were indeed God sent. You said, *"People will buy your book. You don't need all that New York best seller stuff on your cover."* Thanks for believing in my story.

To my intercessors: Cecilia, Rhonda, Colleen, Dwanna, Melissa, Donna Wilcox, Donna Conrad, Mary Lou Couvillion. You have lifted me up for years. Your prayers have been heard on High. Thank you for your faith. You are my most blessed companions on this journey. Julie—My blood sister who encouraged me and told me that my story was worth telling. Tammie—You, dear one, have prayed for me since we were both seven years old. You are such a faith-filled friend. You helped me carry my book dreams, especially the cover, all the way through publishing.

To my Loca sisters: Terri, Glenda, Sharon, Madison, Chelsea, Kathy. You provided the open doors for me to discover a safe place to grow in this beautiful relationship between art and ministry. Loca on Main is the birthing place of me discovering my gifts from God. Thanks for taking a chance on me. You helped me load and unload my art with joy and you serve me so well as I paint and serve others. God truly uses your gifts to bless my soul and my business.

To my soul sister, Ann Younger. God bound our hearts together some fifteen years ago. We shared our hearts and scripture with each other and with women who were all trying to find their way into a lasting relationship with Jesus. I had no idea our artistic worlds would

---

[37] annielaurieward.com

intersect. You have taught me how to live as an artisan and how to improve my art with just a few more strokes of color. But, more importantly, you have modeled for me how to love with depth, width, height and humility. Thanks for being by my side on the rejection days, when I felt my front teeth getting kicked in. Thank you for speaking truth to me and celebrating with me in every single tiny little step forward. God knew I needed you on this journey.

To my customers. To all those along this journey that have bought this art. You are my reason for painting. God wanted to speak to you. I was blessed to be the one He used. Each one of you are a breath of joy and hope within my pathway as an artist. You brought hope and life into my art. I heard you and became better. Without you, I would have never known you felt God through my art. Thank you so much for stopping and listening to the whisper of our Creator.

To the people all over the world making the name of Jesus famous to the ends of the earth. The life you have laid down breathes purpose into my work on the street and in my studio. I am thankful that part of the profits from Acts 1:8 Blessings are used to support this work. My Man and I also continue to go to the nations to tell others of His goodness. My story declares the truth of Acts 1:8 in a victory song.

Made in the USA
Middletown, DE
06 June 2023

32103760R00085